MW00769585

Jungle Harvest

GOD'S WORD TRIUMPHS IN TILA HEARTS

(see page 10)

by
Ruby Scott

Published by Kainos Books, Waxhaw, North Carolina, in 2011.

ISBN 13: 978-0615575490

www.kainosbooks.com

Contents

Acknowledgements 4

Map... 6

1. A Rough Beginning.................................... 7

2. "... Just One More Day" 14

3. "Only 29,999 to Go" 25

4. "I Can't Stand Up and Read" 39

5. "The Black Tortilla Talks"........................ 45

6. Not One Nail Hole..................................... 54

7. "The Owl Killed My Baby" 58

8. Tila Radio Programs.................................. 66

9. The Witch Doctor's Threat........................ 76

10. "Let Me Off the Merry-Go-Round" 83

11. "I Feel Like a King on a Throne".............. 99

12. D-Day 106

13. On a Hilltop Looking Back... 119

14. Amen 127

Photos 139

Acknowledgements

My special thanks to friends all over the country who, through the years, have prayed for Vi and me. Many of you have asked for this story in print. May it encourage your hearts as you realize how abundantly God has answered your prayers.

To Maxine Provence and Mary Brumley who, without my knowledge at the time, saved all of my personal letters written from Mexico. Those letters refreshed memories and brought *Jungle Harvest* into focus.

To Victor Kelly and Faith Blight for their expertise and valuable suggestions in the preparation of the manuscript.

To Viola Warkentin, who not only lived through every experience of the book with me, but for thirty-four years has been my best friend and faithful colleague. I'm grateful for Vi's immeasurable help as she proofread the manuscript, offered suggestions and additions, and typed and edited the finished product. Without Vi's help there would have been no jungle harvest among the Tilas—and no *Jungle Harvest* in your hand today.

But most of all, I want to humbly acknowledge the Tila Indians who, though tucked away in a remote jungle village and completely unknown by the world, have touched and challenged my heart. I witnessed dramatic changes in their lives when they met the Savior who "turned their hearts around and helped them walk down a new trail."

It is my prayer that this book, which chronicles some of the deepest experiences of my life, may bless and encourage you. May it also help each of us realize that many of the world's hidden, seemingly insignificant people—the Felixes, the Rosendos, and the Santiagos—may, in God's omniscience, be among the greatest Christian statesmen of our day.

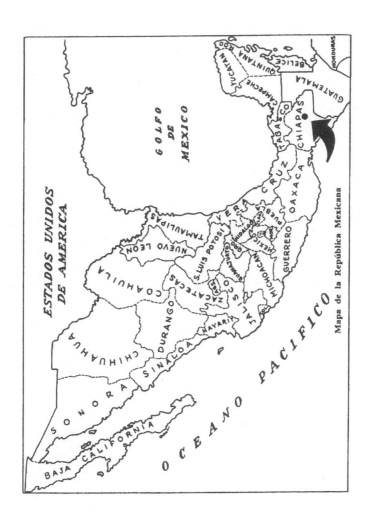

Mapa de la República Mexicana

1
A Rough Beginning

I awakened with a start and for a second couldn't remember where I was. Suddenly my toe touched the mosquito net that hung over my rough board bed like a great parachute. The Indians—that was it! We were in an isolated Tila Chol Indian village in southern Mexico.

The sound, muted as it was, had awakened me. I heard it again. There was no mistaking it or the intention behind it. Someone was trying to break into our house.

My partner, Viola Warkentin, and I were translators with Wycliffe Bible Translators and had just begun our second week in a remote village nestled snugly in the dense tropical jungle in Chiapas, Mexico. There were no roads or electricity or telephones in this village of Chivalito—only people who needed the Scriptures in their own language.

I sat up in bed and stared into the tar-black night. My heart galloped; every beat boomed on my eardrums. We were completely alone among people openly suspicious of our every move, a people with whom we couldn't even communicate. There was no one and no way we could call for help.

I heard the sound again—this time louder. It was voices—voices of men speaking in excited half-whispers. They were all around the house.

I was certain Vi must be awake, but I hadn't heard her move. Then I heard the soft swish of her mosquito net. She crawled out of bed in the darkness and inched toward me.

I reached for my flashlight, but since the wide cracks between the unbeveled boards of the walls would reveal the light to anyone outside, I decided against using it. We tried to whisper. Our frightened voices sounded deep and strange.

There were a few tools and some building materials scattered about the room where we had used them the evening before. I clutched my flashlight tighter. We desperately needed it, but I resisted turning it on. Silently, we groped our way through the darkness to the front door.

A few hours earlier the heavy wooden door had seemed strong and secure. Now it groaned and creaked against the pressure of the mob pushing against it from the outside. I reached out and touched it. I gasped and jerked my hand away. With each push from the outside, it felt as if not just the door but the whole side of the house was about to cave in.

I shook off the terror clamping itself around my throat. We had to find a way to barricade the doors and windows, but I couldn't get one brain cell to work. All I could think about was how many people were out there and what they would do if they got in!

The noise suddenly intensified as the crowd concentrated on our front door. I knew that at any moment the latch would give way and the mob would tumble in! I backed away—and stumbled over a pile of heavy poles I had set aside to make partitions. I quickly grabbed one and inched my way back to the creaking door. I ran my hand over its rough boards searching for the crossbar. I found it and jammed the pole under it. The next mighty shove from the outside drove the other end of the pole into the dirt floor, and the door was secure.

The mob sensed our movements inside. They even seemed to realize what we had done, but they were not ready to give up. They began pushing on the wooden shutters that served as windows. Again with more poles, and still working in the dark, we braced the windows and back door. Then we waited. There was nothing more we could do. We simply stood in the middle of the room wondering what would happen next. There were no beautiful "God will protect and keep you" thoughts swirling around in my head. Instead, I kept thinking: "How did I *ever* get into a situation like this?" There were no thoughts of grandeur—of being a "brave" missionary in the face of imminent danger. All I could think about were my eyes—they hurt from staring into the darkness—and my knees—they felt rubbery. I was just plain scared!

Furious and frustrated, the attackers made several more frenzied attempts to force their way in. Then suddenly all was quiet.

We groped our way back to the bedroom and sat uneasily on the edge of my bed. I tried to swallow, but my throat was too dry. My heart was pounding so hard I thought it must be clearly audible to anyone still outside. Was it over? Had they given up? The sudden quietness was almost as shocking as the noise had been. For several minutes we listened, but there was no further sound. For what seemed a long time, neither of us spoke. It felt good just to sit still and pull ourselves together.

Finally, we found our voices and together thanked the Lord for his protection and care. We reminded each other that God's promises never fail, that every detail of our lives was in his hand—even the unlikely detail of a pile of poles in the house at the right moment.

The staccato beat of my heart slowed. Other thoughts crowded my mind.

At a Women's Missionary Meeting in Yuma, Arizona years before, I had read a prayer letter from Manis and Jane Ruegsegger, Conservative Baptist Home Mission Society missionaries working in a Zapotec Indian tribe in Mexico. In his letter, Manis explained the need to translate the New Testament for people who couldn't understand its message in any language but their own. That need had gripped my heart.

The weeks following, as I went about my duties as a registered nurse in the local hospital, I grappled with the thought that people were being denied the message of the New Testament because it had not been translated into the only language they understood. I decided I could help and applied to the Conservative Baptist Home Mission Society. In January 1953 I became a missionary.

In the summer of that year, I studied linguistics at the University of Oklahoma and was accepted by Wycliffe Bible Translators to work under CBHMS in Mexico. The next year I arrived in southern Mexico to work among the Indians. My dream had come true.

Seated on the edge of the bed in the darkness of the Tila Chol village, my thoughts were suddenly interrupted by a slight noise at the corner of the house. I wanted to see if there were people outside. The cracks between the boards were wide enough, but what if I were to look straight into the eyes of someone looking in?

I listened. All was quiet.

different dialects

Were these Tila Chols really different from the Tumbala Chols with whom Vi and I had spent such a wonderful ten years? I wondered. The Tumbala Chols had at first been suspicious of strangers. They considered the "old way," sprinkled with drunkenness and witchcraft, to be the preferred and only acceptable way of life. Yet as the Tumbala New Testament[1] became available to them, the Lord worked miracles in their lives. Through the years, thousands of Tumbala Chols had become "new creatures in Christ."

---

[1] Translation Team: John and Elaine Beckman, Wilbur and Evelyn Aulie, and Arabelle Anderson Whittaker.

Your great-grandparents

✱Tumbalá was your grandmother Helen Aulie Labosier's childhood home.

We had seen powerful witch doctors become beloved deacons, village drunks become respected leaders, churches built, outgrown, and bigger ones built only to be outgrown again. The literacy classes and Bible studies that Vi and I had conducted were always crowded to capacity. Everyone had wanted to know more of the "God-of-immeasurable-power." Lives had been changed. Villages had been changed.

Vi's whisper brought me back to our present problem. "Surely whoever was out there is gone," she said. She felt her way to her bed and lay down. Sleep was the farthest thing from my mind. I cocked my ear and listened again but heard no further sound.

I held my breath, mustered my courage, and flicked on my flashlight. It was 4:00 A.M. The Tumbala Chols would be getting up about now, I thought. I used to enjoy waking up in a Tumbala village, lying quietly in the predawn darkness and listening as the village began to stir. From first one little thatched-roof home and then another, we would hear a hymn as each family started the day with devotions. No doubt, this very morning, many Tumbala Christians were praying for us even as the Tilas were attempting to break into our house.

And what a house! It also stood as a testimony to the Lord's care for us. Tumbala Christians, in spite of their fear of the machete-wielding Tilas, had come three days by foot and dugout canoe to the Tila area to build this house for us. They had spent weeks cutting huge mahogany trees and hand-sawing them into boards. "Life will be different among the Tilas. You'll have to have a strong house. You can't live in a pole house where the breeze passes through," they said, referring to the Chol-type construction of upright balsa poles tied together with bark.

And the roof. It definitely couldn't be of nice cool thatch such as we had enjoyed in Tumbala villages. "Thatch will burn," they said. The Tumbala Christians who built our house had anticipated our needs.

Still sitting cross-legged in bed, I silently thanked the Lord for board walls and a galvanized metal roof.

All was quiet. I wondered if Vi was asleep.

"Hey, Vi, do you remember that Sunday school teacher I told you about? The one from my home church?"

A soft "uh-huh" came from across the room. Vi was getting sleepy.

"Well," I persisted, "I remember a big discussion he had going once. He said it was absolutely impossible to really trust the Lord and be afraid at the same time. 'The two things can't coexist,' he said. Well, I found out tonight that they can 'coexist' for me. I was *really* scared, and I know I was trusting the Lord!"

There was no sound from Vi's bed.

"Weren't you scared, too?" I asked.

The "uh-huh" was almost inaudible—followed by the sound of deep, even breathing.

I was getting sleepy, too. "Lord," I prayed, "tonight when it looked as if our door were going to cave in, I really wanted to leave here. I wanted to forget I'd ever heard of Chivalito or the Tila Chols. But, Lord, that's not really the way I feel. What I really want to do is to stay here and learn this language so we can tell these people about you. Please, Lord, help us do it."

Then, as if on cue to the rededication that had just welled up in my heart, there was a thunderous crash of stones on the metal roof over our heads. The sound was so sudden and so shattering that I thought I was going to be sick to my stomach.

The Tilas were out there in the dark. They hadn't given up! They were stoning the house. "Lord," I thought, "they're not going to make our task an easy one."

2
"... Just One More Day"

The tug of war began!

The Tilas wanted us out. They felt betrayed by Santiago, the village leader, and all his smooth talk about paper and learning to read little marks on it.

"Bah!" they scoffed. "What does Santiago know about such things? Just because he's been out of the village a few times, he thinks he knows the world!"

"Those foreign women are devils who have tricked him," the women added. "After all, real people don't have sickly pale skin and eyes the color of the sky."

Some were angry at Santiago's decision to let us live in the village. Others were afraid. All agreed that their gods didn't want us in Chivalito. "The gods have given us a sure sign," they said to each other. "Santiago was bitten by a rattlesnake because he allowed women devils to come to Chivalito. Now it's up to us. We must find a way—a very sure way—to get them out. And we must do it soon."

Night after night we were jolted from a fitful sleep by the creaking of a door or window as our "faithful opposition" tried to force it open. The quietness of the night magnified the low mumble of voices as the mob moved from one wooden-shuttered window to another. One deep guttural voice always stood out above the others. We recognized it as that of the short, straggly haired Gregorio. Often his coarse, whispered commands seemed close enough to be in the room with us. Our hearts pounded, fearing that some night a pole would skid on the dirt floor and the mob would tumble in.

Every night as the horror mounted, we firmly decided that if morning ever came, and we were still alive, we would radio the Missionary Aviation Fellowship (MAF) base and ask to be flown out that very day. But even after such long nights, morning always came—and in the daylight the village seemed peaceful. Every morning we watched Gregorio, followed by a woman and several children, hurry along the muddy, overgrown trail on the way to his cornfield.

"I wonder what he must think when he passes our house?" Vi said, as we looked up from our breakfast table.

"I know what I'm thinking," I answered. "I'm wondering if he's going to be back tonight and if our door will hold up!"

We felt trapped between two emotions. We were scared— scared that some night the door latch would fail or that the mob would find some other way to get in. Yet, on the other hand, we felt that if we left the village without learning the language and translating the Bible, the Tilas would never understand God's love.

"Do you think we should leave today?" Vi asked. "Perhaps last night was the last attack. Maybe they'll give up."

"Oh, I don't know," I answered, shaking my head doubtfully. "We thought the same thing every day last week." We sat quietly drinking coffee as we watched several men with their heads down hurry along the trail in front of our house. "But maybe you're right," I added thoughtfully. "The Lord has protected us. And they have to give up someday. Let's not leave today. Let's stay just one more day."

But night after endless night, the attacks continued. Night after night our knees turned to rubber as we stared into the darkness and prayed that the doors would stand another night's battering without flying open! Night after night we

15

made up our minds to leave—and every morning we decided to stay "just one more day."

One day melted into another. The night visits became fewer. Finally, after about three weeks, they stopped.

There were also other changes. Mothers stopped scolding children whose curiosity made them brave enough to come into our house. We listened and jotted down words as they touched and exclaimed about things they had never seen. With speech punctuated by shy giggles, they repeated words and phrases until we could say them to their satisfaction.

The women's hostility faded. They spent more and more time standing outside the glassless windows, watching our every move. Occasionally one or another added a word to our rapidly growing vocabulary. We collected words and phrases on our notepads as eagerly as a miser hoards money. In the evening when the last curious set of eyes left the window, we closed the shutters and turned on a gasoline lantern as we eagerly sorted through that day's collection of words and phrases to record them for future reference.

Our knowledge of Tumbala Chol helped, and soon we understood whole sentences. A recurring remark, always accompanied by a worried look and followed by a rapid exchange that we couldn't follow, was the women's concern that maybe we had really come to steal their husbands. Although we could understand most of what they said, we didn't yet have sufficient vocabulary to attempt an answer.

"Someday it'll be fun to let them know how much of all this we understood," Vi said with a sparkle in her eyes.

"Yeah," I agreed. "I can see you now—running off with little short Honorato and living 'happily ever after' in his leaky, thatched-roof hut!"

"He wouldn't be 'happy ever after' if he had to eat tortillas the way I pat them," she laughed.

We knew that someday the women would understand our reason for being there. But, for now, we must collect and record every word possible.

Mimicking our English became a great source of village fun. The youngsters enjoyed crawling around on their hands and knees, letting out a few "oinks" and "squeals" as they mimicked. We joined in the laughter and even repeated English words for them. It became an exciting game to "exchange words." The women often joined in the fun. Each evening we had an ever-growing harvest of Tila words, all hoarded toward a wonderful day when we would be able to tell the Tilas about the Lord.

Parental warning that we had a large pot in which to boil children began to dim, and several children became regular visitors. They hooted with laughter when we attempted to say something in Tila but patiently corrected us until we said it "straight."

Weeks stretched into months, and our conversational skill in Tila grew at a gratifying rate. The people noticed and seemed pleased. "I taught them that word," they would say with a triumphant tilt of the head.

The flow of visitors also increased. Sometimes they just walked in, watched us for a few minutes, and then left without a word. More often, however, they would goad each other on to talk with us. Sometimes they offered to wash our clothes or carry a pail of water. They giggled and were pleased when we understood and responded.

Our battery-operated radio became a big attraction. In the cool of the evening, men and boys sat around on tree trunks in our yard and visited among themselves as they listened to music. They, too, seemed eager to share their world with us as they identified night birds that swooped overhead or trilled from nearby trees.

We were always amazed at the size and variety of bizarre-looking jungle insects and bugs attracted to our lantern. Some had a three- to four-inch wingspan. Even the men squirmed when one thudded against their faces or necks. I turned up my collar. I certainly didn't want one down my blouse!

The men laughed as the boys darted around, caught them, then patiently repeated the name until we wrote it on our notepad. Men and boys alike crowded at our elbow when we pulled out a pencil to "capture" a word. They were amazed that marks on paper could represent words and that we could look at those marks and repeat the word correctly. They would reach over, touch the marks, and slowly shake their heads. "*C'otyajax*," they would say. "*Noj c'otyajax.*"

After the "lesson," we often winced as the boys pulled the wings off the insects and shoved them deep in their pockets. A pocketful of toasted insects made a tasty snack when the boys got home.

Santiago, who had recovered from the snakebite, occasionally joined the men. Their brief hostility toward him had vanished, and he was respected once again as village leader. Since Santiago spoke Spanish, he was the only one with whom we could converse freely. But his strength was limited and his visits usually short.

One evening after the others left, Santiago stayed. He seemed to feel much better and was in a chatty mood. In Spanish, flavored heavily with his Tila accent, he told us his dream of having a school in Chivalito.

As leader of the village, Santiago had once made a trip all the way to Tuxtla, the state capital. "People in the 'big world' can look at marks on paper and say them, just like you do," he said. He picked up a stick and idly poked at a hole in the ground. Then, looking at us as if confiding a deep secret, added, "I want my son Margarito to be able to do that too."

Vi, a quiet, slim schoolteacher from Meade, Kansas, had invested sixteen years in preparing literacy materials and teaching Tumbala Chol Indians to read. Through the years she had taught thousands in many scattered villages.

She found her voice before I did! "Yes," she said, "Five-year-old Margarito will learn. And not only Margarito, but you and many others. And you will also learn to hold this 'special stick' and make marks on paper, just as Ruby and I do."

Vi's confidence was reassuring. Even to me.

Santiago pulled a flashlight from a frayed pocket, picked up his walking stick and, with a soft *"muchas gracias,"* disappeared down the trail.

After Santiago left, Vi and I continued to sit in the cool, dark yard letting our hearts bask in the hope and joy reignited by that visit. Could these be the same people who only months before had scorned Santiago's "highfalutin idea" of reading? Had he somehow convinced them of their need to learn? Yes, we believed he had. "You know," I said laughing, "my dad would have referred to Santiago as the type of man who could 'talk the Eskimos into buying snow.'"

Another hour slipped past, and a huge orange moon slid into the dark sky. We enjoyed the night sounds as monkeys chattered and crickets filled the jungle with song.

It was late. We reluctantly folded our chairs and stood for a moment looking out over the sleeping village. Much was happening. God was at work. We bowed our heads and committed ourselves and the future of the village into God's hands. By faith we could see hundreds of Tilas reading—not only reading but eagerly reading the New Testament translated into their language!

At the moment that goal seemed far away. We were still struggling with a few details of the final analysis of the

19

language and the formation of an alphabet. But with God at work in the hearts of the Tilas, we were ready to expect the impossible. After all, only six months before we huddled in fear and darkness as, night after night, men beat on our doors and windows. Tonight that darkness seemed soft and friendly. Some of the men who had made up those terrifying mobs were now friends and had spent the evening sitting around our house visiting with us.

A half hour later, we crawled into bed and dropped our mosquito nets around us. Our hearts danced with the thought of the entire Tila tribe—thirty thousand men, women, and children—each with a book in his hand, reading!

At breakfast the next morning, all we could talk about was Santiago's visit and its implications.

"You know, the way the men and boys crowded around and watched as we wrote Tila words last night, maybe they'll all want to learn," I said.

"Yes. Perhaps Chivalito will turn into another Suclumpa," Vi said, referring to a Tumbala village where we had lived five years before.

"Wow! That would be great. Of all the Tumbala villages we lived in, Suclumpa was my favorite." I said.

"Mine, too," she agreed. "Do you remember old Sebastian? He really had a hard time learning to read—but he did it."

"He sure did! Remember the big surprise he had for us on our last night there?" I said, smiling.

"Yes," Vi said, as we remembered the happy months spent in Sebastian's village.

Sebastian was older than most of the men in those evening reading classes. None had ever read. In a few days, however, the others learned the six Tumbala vowels and were ready for the big step of attaching consonants to them to form syllables. Sebastian, who was still struggling with the rudiments of holding his vowel chart right side up, watched from a corner. To him, the vowels looked just as good upside down as right side up. How could one really ever tell the difference? The other men in the class respected Sebastian and often gently turned his paper around.

The rest of the class quickly progressed to syllables, then words, and to easy reading material. Sebastian trailed far behind. He never missed a class and always applied himself diligently. But it seemed that no matter how hard he tried, his mind just couldn't "grab the truth" of marks on paper.

After weeks of study with little progress, Sebastian became discouraged. We had only four months left in his village. He would never read by then. He desperately wanted to learn so he could read the Scripture that was being translated and would soon become a book. But what good was that book to one whose mind couldn't stretch over the marks on each page?

The next evening as Vi and I arrived at the balsa-pole school, we were met by a group of enthusiastic young men ready to tackle another night of classes. Sebastian sat alone on his backless bench, lost in thought. He idly fingered his syllable chart as his bare toes dug little holes in the dirt floor. His face was a mask of discouragement. He would give up. He just couldn't learn!

I sat down to help him. For a moment his eyes strayed to the newly published Scripture portion on the bench beside me. Our eyes met, and he quickly turned away and seemed to be studying his toes. I reached over, opened the portion to James 1:5 and quietly read in Tumbala: *"Dios mi yuq'uen i na'tubal majchical jach ml c'ajtin. Ma'an mi wis chuquiben mu' bu i c'ajtiben."* The promise was there. It was true and

21

everlasting. God would give wisdom to anyone who asked for it.

Sebastian quickly laid down his reading chart and slipped out of class. My heart ached for him as he made his way over a moonless jungle trail to his little thatched-roof hut.

The next evening as the class gathered, my eyes kept straying to the door watching for Sebastian. He didn't come. Nor the next night. Nor the next. The Book he longed to enjoy was going to be closed to him.

A week passed and we didn't see Sebastian. Then late one afternoon, I heard a soft greeting and turned to welcome him. In a humdrum manner, he "visited" for ten minutes, while my mind whirled, trying to decide what he really wanted. He stepped to the door and glanced out. No one was in sight. Then pulling a long piece of straw from our thatched roof and studying it carefully as he talked, he said, "My heart is hungry to read God's Word, but I can't grab the truth of marks on paper. I work in my field all day, and the hot sun scatters my head. At night I'm tired and my head won't come together. Maybe I could learn if you taught me early in the morning before I go to work."

He searched my face for understanding. I nodded.

"That's a good idea. I'll be glad to teach you every morning an hour before the sun wakes up," I said.

With a soft touch of a handshake and a shy smile, he disappeared down the trail.

I stood in the open door enjoying the towering philodendron and the sweet smell of coffee blossoms. I bowed my head. "Thank you, Lord, for letting me be here. And thank you that you are going to help Sebastian read your Word!"

The next morning, in the velvet blackness before dawn, I was awakened by Sebastian's voice outside our little one-room hut. I fumbled for a flashlight. It was 4:00 A.M. I struggled into my clothes, which were under the mosquito net with me. I climbed out of bed, flashlight in hand, shook out my shoes to dislodge any snakes or scorpions that might be there, and lit the gasoline lantern. Morning classes began.

When it was light enough to see the trail, Sebastian went to work. He came home at noon so his head could "cool off" for an afternoon session; then he returned later for the regular evening class. His "scattered head" began to come together and "memory stretched over the letters." In a month be had mastered simple reading material and was on the way to his big goal—reading God's Word.

When we left the village three months later, as a special "gift" to us, Sebastian stood before a packed church and in a loud, clear voice read James 1:2-8. Old people leaned forward to catch every word. The young men, who had patiently helped and encouraged him in his long struggle, smiled and nodded as he read each verse. Then, his voice trembling with emotion, Sebastian thanked the Lord for sending us to "open God's Word" for him. "Lord, please reward them," he prayed.

Tears clouded my eyes. The joy that wreathed his wrinkled old face was rich reward!

We moved to other Tumbala villages and eventually to the Tilas. Occasionally we heard about Sebastian who became a well-loved pastor among the Tumbalas.

Reminiscing about Sebastian brought pleasant memories as we turned our thoughts to the challenge of preparing materials and starting classes in Chivalito.

Vi looked at me across the breakfast table as a slow smile gathered at the corners of her lips. "You know, I believe the Lord is going to do great things for the Tilas, just as he did among the Tumbalas. Aren't you glad he helped us stay here 'just one more day'?"

3
"Only 29,999 to Go"

As we neared the end of our second year in Chivalito, the frustration of language learning had faded. We spoke Tila as quickly and naturally as English.

School was in full swing, and the students loved their new Tila primers and workbooks. Already, some had advanced to simple reading material.

When attendance climbed from five to forty-eight, the village got excited about "knowing paper." They gathered poles from the jungle and lashed them together with sturdy bark, and built a second school. Two men spent weeks building twenty desks like the ones they had seen in the market town of Salto de Agua. They copied every detail— even the bright green color. When the job was completed, the village gathered for a tamale dinner to celebrate their new school.

At first, school was restricted to boys. "Girls are useful for washing clothes or picking coffee," the parents agreed, "but there is no reason for them to waste time learning marks on paper."

Little girls in Chivalito responded as girls all over the world do, they fussed and cried and three months later won "equal rights." A prized pencil clutched in one hand, black hair tied back in a bright strip of cloth, they trotted along behind a brother on their way to school.

As school progressed, I slowly got used to sticky little hands constantly patting and touching me. My fair skin was in such stark contrast to their beautiful coppery tones that they never tired of running their hands over my arms and neck. My curly blond hair was a never-ending source of wonder and drew little fingers like a magnet. Each had to feel it to prove that it was real. Yes, it did grow out of my scalp just like theirs!

Even so, they concluded, it was different from "real hair." Since the weather was hot, I kept it cut very short. 'The children often commented to one another, "Look at our poor Ruby. Her hair just won't grow." When they discovered that I regularly cut it, the little fingers really flew. I soon realized that they were checking for lice—the only acceptable reason for a woman to cut her hair.

One morning I sat at the table with ten little ones, my attention focused on a reading problem. Suddenly, little Jorge, sitting beside me, affectionately patted my upper arm. The reading problem solved, I shifted my attention back to Jorge and realized the "pat" wasn't from affection. He and several others were trying to guess how many pounds of lard my upper arm could produce.

I thought of my friends at home who insisted that I was getting much too thin at 130 pounds.

Each day school dismissed at noon, and the children scampered off to work in their cornfields. That seemed to be the women's cue to visit. Often several leaned on the Dutch door that separated our front room from the dining area. Accompanied by wry faces and wrinkled noses, they kept a running commentary on what we ate.

"Look at Vi's fork," Chula exclaimed. "How does she keep from stabbing her lips?" Fascinated, they watched it make its safe trip from plate to mouth. They concluded the fork was a "dangerous tool" and that it was much safer to eat with a nice soft tortilla.

The ladies fingered and admired our dresses. They often commented on how long it must take to sew with such tiny stitches. We tried to explain the sewing machine. They shrugged and mumbled to each other. "One sews with fingers. How can a machine have fingers?"

On our next trip to Tuxtla we bought a sturdy treadle sewing machine. The ladies quickly learned, and the machine whirred for hours at a time. "Now we sew like foreign women," they laughed.

All Tila women wore a simple one-style-only dress. Soon the most daring copied our variety of necklines and sleeves. The old women scowled and predicted dire consequences, but the men approved. Tila styles took a great leap forward.

Washing clothes was a problem for us, since all our water was carried from a deep hole in the ground a five-minute walk away. We knew the women washed in a nearby stream, and though we were intrigued by their methods, we didn't want to follow them. They stood knee-deep in the water and, after generously soaping each piece with strong bar soap, swung it above their heads, and slapped it against a large rock. Often the repeated slap, slap of clothes against rock resounded from several streams. Although their clothes didn't have zippers or buttons, I wasn't surprised that they didn't last long. There were no bed linens to wash since people slept on grass mats on the ground. Towels were also unknown to them.

We were pleased when Basilia and Adela began to vie for a chance to wash our clothes. That would solve the problem of sheets and towels, but we were reluctant to send our dresses and undies to be beaten on the rocks. "Please," they begged, "let us wash everything for you. We'll be careful."

Vi shrugged and gave me her "what-do-you-think?" look.

"It's fine with me," I said. "Washday certainly isn't my favorite day of the week! Besides, that will give them a chance to finger our dresses—without us in them."

"OK," she said with a laugh. "That will probably be the end of our buttons and zippers, but I guess we can live without them. They do."

She divided the wash into two equal piles, each with a bar of laundry soap.

Basilia and Adela grabbed up their bundles, slung them to their backs and, bare feet flying, headed for the stream.

We stood shaking our heads as the girls disappeared down the narrow trail. "I doubt if they really like to wash clothes," Vi said. "Perhaps they are just looking for a way to say 'thank you' for sewing machines or reading classes."

A few weeks later, to our chagrin, we discovered that each washday a group of women met and had a "style show" before washing our clothes. We were appalled but decided not to object; they were having fun and solving our washday blues at the same time.

We devoted afternoons to a women's reading class, and in the evening, it was the men's turn. All pupils, whether six or sixty, had to start with vowels and consonants in the strange and wonderful adventure of "knowing paper."

Often when there was a full moon, the men stayed after class to look at pictures in the *National Geographic* magazine and ask searching questions about the outside world. Occasionally we talked about the Lord and the Book we had come to translate. Some seemed mildly interested; others changed the subject.

Night after night, as soon as the class left, we spread out our commentaries and concentrated on translation. Slowly the Gospel of Mark began to "speak Tila."

One evening we read several verses to Santiago, Felix, and Venancio, who stayed after class to visit. They listened attentively. "Is that the message from the sun, our holy father?" Venancio asked.

"No. It is from the Almighty God who made the sun," Vi answered.

Santiago, in his usual straightforward way, said, "If there is a God greater than the sun, we should listen to him."

"Yes," I agreed. Then, picking up my Bible, I continued, "It is his message that is written in this book. This is the message we came to write down for you."

With their encouragement, we decided to set a time each Sunday afternoon when we would publicly read the chapter we were translating. Anyone interested in hearing God's Word was invited.

Sunday services began!

A few people gathered in the school each Sunday as Vi or I read the verses. Most of them enjoyed the get-together but ignored us as we read. They talked loudly about their cornfields, shared snake stories, or discussed some other subject. Each week a different group came. We were discouraged by their apparent lack of interest. In spite of what we said, everyone knew, of course, that the sun is our holy father and the moon our holy mother. The message of Mark was very strange! It was all right with them if we wanted to spend hours writing the Bible in Tila. They knew it wasn't really true!

But as the weeks wore on, we discovered that some who came again and again and usually talked the loudest were doing it as a guise so others wouldn't guess they were really listening to the message about God.

Teenaged Petrona frequently came to services with several younger brothers and sisters. She was unusually

29

pretty with a petite, round face, shiny black hair that reached to her waist, and large beautiful eyes. After she became our friend, we realized Petrona was from the dreaded Cruz clan. Her father, Pascual, had murdered a man and then crushed his head with rocks. An older brother, in a fit of anger, had slashed open his wife's abdomen with his razor-sharp machete.

Petrona, forbidden to come to reading classes, showed keen interest in the Sunday messages. Gradually I noticed that she also had another interest—Felix, handsome and ever-smiling sitting in a back corner. Although usually noisy, he always had an eye on Petrona. She was aware of his attention and enjoyed it.

Two months later the village buzzed with a new story. Pascual had sold Petrona to Moises, an old man in the village of Santa Lucia. Old Moises, who already had a wife and two daughters older than Petrona, had offered Pascual a high bride price: a kilo of salt (2.2 pounds), 3 kilos of sugar, 2 1/2 yards of cloth, and 8 quarts of liquor. Pascual accepted the offer. The deal was struck. Moises would now have two wives.

Petrona cried and begged her father not to take her away. He refused to listen. He had drunk liquor with Moises; the agreement was final! That afternoon he took her to Santa Lucia and left her in the one-room hut with Moises, his wife, and four of their children.

A drunken revelry went on for hours. Before morning Petrona was forced to become his wife.

The next morning Petrona ran away and returned home. Pascual, still drunk, grabbed a stick to beat her. She fled again. Chula, our neighbor, befriended Petrona, but the next day when a search was begun, Chula's fear of the murderous Pascual overwhelmed her, and she brought Petrona to our house.

"Hide her!" she demanded as she and Petrona dashed to our back door. "Pascual is coming—and he's drunk! Open your door. Quick! You have the only safe house in Chivalito. Hide her before they get here."

Petrona's eyes pleaded with us to let her in. We opened the door and hid her in the closet, the only out-of-sight spot in our house.

That night Petrona's mother came and begged us to help her daughter. "I am afraid of what her father will do when he is angry," she said.

We wanted to help Petrona but didn't know what Mexican law said about such cases. Did Petrona have a right to run away from a man she had been forced to marry? The law certainly didn't condone multiple wives, but would we be liable if we helped her escape? We decided to hide her until we could find answers.

That night we read translated Scripture portions with Petrona and prayed for wisdom. She enjoyed the Word, and for the first time since her arrival in our house, talked with us. "I want to marry Felix," she confided. "I don't want Moises. He's older than my father, and his wife and children laugh at me. My mother likes Felix, too, but he didn't offer as much liquor as old Moises did."

For two frustrating days, while Petrona huddled in our closet, we contacted Mexican friends and acquaintances in our search for answers. We were finally assured that the law protects a woman from being forced to marry or live with a man against her will. We sent the word to Pascual and Moises. Instead of being intimidated by Mexican law, Pascual was furious at our intervention. "So that's where she's hiding," he bellowed. "I'll go down there and tear the metal roof off that house and take her out!"

31

The next day we heard that Pascual bought kerosene to throw on our house and burn us out. We doubted he would have the nerve; Petrona was sure he would. With each new story, she huddled on the floor and shook with fear. She begged us to protect her from her father.

The following afternoon, Flora, who lived in Petrona's end of the village, came to buy medicine. As she left, she nonchalantly mentioned that Moises, Pascual, and Petrona's older brother were on the trail headed for our house. "They are drunk and have their machetes," she added.

In a few minutes seven-year-old Margarito, who seemed to know every move that went on in Chivalito, flashed through the door and announced, "They're coming! They are at the cross-trail!" He darted out the back door and ducked into the banana patch. He, as usual, wouldn't miss a second of any excitement.

Petrona was shaken by Flora's information, but Margarito's statement was devastating! She had desperately hoped Pascual would not break into our house and take her forcefully. That hope was gone; he was almost there. She sat cross-legged on the floor, sobbing and shaking with fear. We sat down beside her, read more promises from God's Word, and prayed with her. "God is almighty and has promised to never leave us nor forsake us," I assured her. "He will take care of us." She wanted to believe me, but the terror she felt toward her father and brother was more real to her than God's promises. I sat still, prayed silently, and held her hand.

A half hour passed. Margarito bobbed in and out of the banana patch but kept an eye on the trail. A long fifteen minutes later, his patience badly frayed, he scampered over the trail to see what had happened to the three men.

Minutes later he dashed to our door with the news. "They stopped at Adrian's house to have another drink," he laughed. "Now they are all stretched out on his floor, asleep.

Their mouths are hanging open like this, and they are snoring," he said, as he cocked his head to one side, opened his mouth, and made a deep rasping noise. A second later, he dashed home to tell Santiago the news.

Vi and I looked at each other, relieved. Petrona smiled— the first time in days. Her smile seemed to say, "Maybe—just maybe—the foreign women's God does have power. Maybe his word is true."

Chivalito passed a quiet night.

Few people were willing to get involved in anything that had to do with the murderous Cruz clan. One man, however, promised to go to Salto and report the problem to the local authorities. We sent word to Pascual. "We intend to report you to the Mexican authorities unless you immediately settle this matter with Moises. They will take action against you."

"No authorities have ever come to Chivalito," he flared. "Do those foreign devils think they can scare me with their empty words?" He spat at a tree trunk and scorned the message.

The next morning, Valerio, who had promised to go to Salto for us, passed by on his way to the field.

"Hello, Valerio," Vi called. "What happened? You said you were going to Salto today."

He paused, as if thinking of an excuse. "Well, I changed my mind," he answered lamely. "I don't have my loads ready. Maybe I'll go next week."

"Next week?" I groaned in disbelief as Valerio hurried out of sight. "Next week! We told Pascual to settle the matter, or we would send word to the authorities today."

Our words, indeed, sounded "empty."

I glanced at my watch. Eight o'clock. Our scheduled 7:30 A.M. radio communication with the MAF base had slipped past again—the second day in a row. I sighed and shrugged. "They're not going to like that very much," I said, looking off into space. We both felt the tension and uncertainty of the Petrona problem.

At about ten o'clock, we heard a familiar roar. It sounded like the MAF plane, but we had not asked for a flight. We stepped to the door and looked up. There it was—the little red and white "metal bird." The pilot made a wide circle over the village and then rumbled to a stop on the airstrip in front of our house. Pilot Gene Congdon and a college friend, who was visiting, climbed out to greet us.

"Hi, ladies," Gene said, with a worried look. "Are you all right? You haven't answered our call in two days, so we decided we'd better come see what's going on."

"Oh, we're OK. Just forgot to turn the radio on," I apologized. "We've had a lot going on."

The arrival of the plane always attracted a crowd, but that morning the crowd was unusually large. Our threat to report Pascual to the authorities had apparently made the rounds. With a quick glance I noticed Pascual slouching down on the outer edge of the chattering crowd.

All the people knew the pilot, but this morning their full attention was focused on the visitor. Who was the nicely dressed young man with the tiny mustache? We were obviously telling him all about Petrona who was still hidden in our house. "Yes! That must be the president of Mexico!" they concluded.

We continued talking with Gene and his friend without realizing that the crowd was assuring Pascual that we had "very strong words." "See. That's the real president of Mexico, and he has come to put you in jail."

Someone giggled loudly, and I glanced up to see old Pascual make a fast retreat into the thick jungle on the side of the airstrip. Within minutes he was on his way to Santa Lucia to talk to Moises. Moises who had seen the plane fly overhead was on his way to Chivalito. They met in mid-trail. "The president of Mexico has come to Chivalito to put us in jail," Pascual exclaimed. "I thought they were lying. I didn't think he would really come. But he's here. He's in Chivalito—and they're probably looking for us right now!"

The two men sat down on a mossy rock and made quick plans. Pascual agreed to give Moises another daughter in exchange for Petrona. Lucita wasn't as young or pretty and had no objections to living with Moises as a second wife. The bargain was struck. Pascual gave Moises a turkey to repay part of the liquor he had drunk.

Petrona was free—but still afraid to go home.

The next day Petrona's mother came as if to take her home. We quietly told them good-bye and watched as they hurried down the trail. "What do you think will happen when they get home," I wondered.

"Maybe nothing," Vi said, "if Pascual is sober."

"I sure hope he's sober," I mused.

Felix, Petrona, and her mother had other plans. Unknown to us, Petrona's mother took her to meet Felix at a pre-arranged place on the trail. The two were together at last.

Pascual was sober and received the news calmly.

Punctuated with the usual number of murders and machete fights, the weeks slipped past. The rains turned the jungle into a sauna bath, miry with ankle-deep mud and teeming with mosquitoes. The men brought wet cornhusks to class and burned them as a smudge. A variety of jungle night-flying bugs sent us scurrying under our nets to do our late-night studying. The heat and humidity seemed unbearable. We needed a vacation.

35

The cool mountainous town of San Cristobal de Las Casas provided the perfect answer. For three days, we read, slept, and ate. Gradually we relaxed and village problems slipped into perspective and energy returned. For another three weeks we became typical tourists as we enjoyed nice restaurants and poked around in quaint shops and markets.

Vacation over, we were happy to return to Chivalito and the challenges of village life.

An hour after our arrival, a very pale Felix struggled up to our door, stood hugging the doorpost, and asked for medicine. He untied a bloody rag and held out his hand, palm up. I gasped as three fingers fell limply backwards. The tendons were completely severed.

"Will you sew it up for me, like you sewed up Jeronimo's leg?" he asked.

I took a deep breath and put my hand under his to support the dangling fingers. He winced as I examined the deep two-inch gash.

"No, Felix," I said, slowly shaking my head. "This wound is different. Your hand has little rubbers in it that make the fingers move. Those rubbers are cut. We need to go to a hospital and ask a doctor to sew them back together. If we don't, you'll never be able to move your fingers again."

Felix slumped in a chair, his head hanging. Finally, he looked up and spoke. "No, Ruby. I need to tell you how I did this. I was drunk last night and fell on my liquor bottle. It's my fault my fingers won't move. You shouldn't pity me."

It took some convincing, but two hours later Felix and I watched the village drop away beneath us as the MAF plane took off toward Tuxtla and a three-hour tendon repair. After surgery, Dr. Rojas put a cast on Felix's arm from fingertips to elbow. The next day he cut a window in it, so I could tend the wound and take out the stitches. As he told us good-bye, he gave instructions to remove the cast in a month and start therapy on the fingers. A big order for an R.N., but not too big for an R.N. and the Lord.

The wound healed well and I began the time-consuming therapy. For an hour, three times a day, Felix sat with his hand in a basin of warm water as I massaged the stiff fingers and talked to him about the Lord.

Two months later we neared the end of therapy sessions. Felix's hand was better; his fingers moved well. But even more thrilling was his deep interest in God's Word.

Although a struggling reader, he took home a carbon copy of the Gospel of Mark. He read to Petrona, and they discussed the Word together. They especially enjoyed the account of Jesus calming the storm.

The next day at our therapy session, Felix said, "You know, Ruby, we have always believed that the sun is our holy father. He makes our corn grow, so we don't go hungry. But our god couldn't stop the wind from blowing or the rain from falling like Jesus did.

"And besides," he continued, "the sun doesn't know us by name. He doesn't love us. He couldn't have made my fingers move again. But Jesus did. He even made a man's legs work, so the man could walk again.

"Petrona and I talked about it last night. I believe what you've been saying is true. Jesus is really God. He has power that can't be measured. I want him to take the sin from my heart. I want to ask him to turn my heart around and make it walk on the straight path. I want to do it now."

Quietly, without fanfare, Felix bowed his head and prayed.

As Felix prayed, I sat very still—afraid to move. Afraid I would awaken from a dream. But this was no dream. It had

37

happened. The Lord had written the very first Tila name in the Book of Life!

Tears filled my eyes. The early weeks of nighttime terror, the months of struggle with language learning, the tensions and frustration of village living—all these melted away to nothing. Felix had accepted the Lord!

That night, too thrilled to sleep, my mind reached out to all the far-flung villages with their total population of 30,000 Tilas. Would those people's hearts be as hard as Chivalito's had been only two short years ago? Even so, they all needed to understand the life-changing message Felix had just embraced.

I closed my eyes. It was late. I must go to sleep.

Suddenly, I giggled and not even the blackness of night could stifle it. I sat up, forgetting that Vi might be asleep, and called, "Hey Vi, you know what? Isn't it wonderful? Now there are only 29,999 more Tilas who still need the Lord."

The countdown had started!

4
"I Can't Stand Up and Read"

Rosendo was the village drunk. In the three years we had lived in Chivalito, we had seen him sober only two or three times. His frequent drunken brawls occasioned the kind of excitement on which the village thrived. One of those incidents happened in the shade between our house and the school.

Late one afternoon Vi and I heard loud talking and stepped to the window. Several men had gathered and were watching Rosendo and an equally drunk Jose sashay back and forth, threatening each other with machetes. They inched closer and closer together. I shuddered and closed my eyes. Suddenly Vi grabbed my arm and gasped. I looked up, expecting the worst.

Rosendo's machete had flicked out and nicked Jose's arm. Jose looked at the blood and lost all desire to fight. He fled as fast as his drunken, wobbly legs would allow. Rosendo stood still for a minute as his liquor-befuddled brain sorted out a decision. Then, yelling Tila words not in our vocabulary, he decided to finish the fight and pursued Jose. As he neared the end of the airstrip, his machete flashing in the sun, he was fast closing the gap. I turned my head. I knew all too well what would happen when that machete found its mark!

The crowd was quiet with every person anticipating the bloody result. Then, accompanied by a roar of laughter and wild hoots and yells, the crowd began slapping each other on the back. I chanced a quick look.

Rosendo had disappeared. Jose was staggering up the trail beyond the single log that spanned a five-foot-wide muddy ditch at the end of the airstrip. Then I saw Rosendo. He had fallen off the log bridge and was struggling to free himself from the waist-deep gooey mess. Muddy and embarrassed, he lost all interest in pursuit.

But that was three months ago. Tonight a sober Rosendo came to listen as Felix and I continued work on the Gospel of Mark. Wide-eyed and leaning forward with his arms sprawled across the table, he didn't miss a word.

An hour and a half later, still as silent as a sphinx, Rosendo and Felix left. As the door closed behind them, we heard the stored-up questions tumble out. Vi and I prayed silently for both men as we watched the two flashlights slowly bob along the trail and out of sight.

"That was really a good session tonight," Vi said with a smile as we turned our attention to putting away the books.

"Yeah, Felix was really sharp," I replied, "but it's hard to know if Rosendo understands anything when all he does is nod and grunt."

Vi laughed. "That's all he does here," she said, "but I'll bet he picks Felix's brain every step of the way home."

Rosendo and Felix had been neighbors for years. After that fight beside the school, Felix had again talked with Rosendo about the Lord. "God's Word feels good to my heart. Come with me tomorrow night and listen for yourself as Ruby and Vi read it," he said. Rosendo wasn't interested.

Felix didn't give up. His bubbly personality and quick sense of humor made him the center of any group. The new facet of a deep spiritual commitment added to his maturity without diminishing his popularity. He shared his faith easily and naturally. Over the next two months, Rosendo often heard Felix speak of the Lord and the Bible that Vi and I were translating. Rosendo wasn't interested in a "foreign" god—but he was curious about the changes he saw in Felix's life. He began to listen and ask questions.

"Is it really true that God is alive and we can talk to him?" he asked.

"Yes. God is alive. His words are in the book that Ruby and Vi are writing in our language. Come with me tonight and listen for yourself"

Rosendo shrugged indecisively, "Well, I don't know. Maybe I will."

That was the beginning. Night after night Rosendo accompanied Felix as he helped us revise the Gospel of Mark. He listened attentively but seldom spoke. If asked a question, he would wave a hand and say, "Felix knows."

Felix was an unusual young man, especially chosen by the Lord for the translation task. He had an insatiable desire for the Word but a tenacity that made him stick to a verse until he was sure that every detail was perfect. At the completion of each group of verses, Felix would sit back, cup his hands behind his head and, with a satisfied smile, listen as I read the portion. "Ah," he would say, now God's Word speaks Tila. That's beautiful." Rosendo would grunt and nod throughout the reading. "Yes," he would add, "the words are coming out straight."

In spite of the progress made at the translation desk, we often felt that the more important session of the evening took place on the trail home as Felix answered Rosendo's questions and discussed the implications of the new things they learned. Rosendo agreed that the Word definitely "felt good" to his heart.

Rosendo and Felix became close friends and often went to Salto together. Felix's presence helped Rosendo refuse the liquor offered by his drunken friends. "Ha," a friend would taunt, "look at Rosendo turning into a woman!" Another, waving a bottle under his nose would add, "Yeah, maybe we should buy him a dress."

Vi and I watched as the Lord helped Rosendo. Weeks slipped by without liquor. His friends began to notice changes in him. On his trips to Salto, they watched in amazement as he bypassed the bar and stopped at the corner vender to buy sweet rolls to bring home to his children. The men were puzzled. They also noticed that since he wasn't always sleeping off a drunk, he spent more time working in his field. He bought cloth on his trips to Salto, and Lupita made dresses and shirts for their children. Yes, Rosendo was different.

The villagers enjoyed taunting him publicly, but secretly they wondered if their mundane lives could ever become as quiet and content as Rosendo's.

"What do you think about Rosendo these days?" Juan asked one morning as he and Aureliano struggled over the muddy trail.

Aureliano slipped, caught his balance, and sat down wearily on a protruding tree trunk. "Oh, I don't know," he answered. "Whatever happened to Felix last year seems to be happening to Rosendo, too. They don't even get angry when we taunt them! I've been wondering if it's really true what they say about God. Or maybe they've found some new medicine that has made them stop drinking."

"Yeah, it's strange," Juan said, slowly shaking his head. "Very strange. Felix is young and attracted to new ideas, but Rosendo is old like us."

One by one, the men began looking for a way to talk with Rosendo alone. They wanted to know what had changed his life.

Rosendo couldn't give them a theological explanation, but he could give them a simple, straightforward answer—an answer that made them even more curious about the new life he was living. "God isn't the sun up in the sky as we have always thought," he said. "He's a person, and he has grabbed my heart and turned it toward the straight trail."

The dramatic changes in Rosendo's life that caught the interest of the village made it easier for Felix to talk about the One who changes lives. Quietly, he continued to share the message.

The Gospel of Mark now spoke good Tila, and attendance at the Sunday services increased. A few learned the words to the four hymns and began to sing along with us. To please those who had "conquered paper," we enlarged the hymnal to ten hymns and made copies for all who could read. They clutched their bright blue copy of *"La' Lac Cuye' Dios"* and shyly glanced around to see if others noticed their hymnbooks. The singing improved. Sunday services came to life!

One Sunday evening as Vi and I washed the supper dishes, she said, "You know, I think we should stop leading the church services."

"Yeah, I've been thinking that, too," I agreed. "If we do it too long, they'll get used to us and think they can't do it themselves. Felix reads well, and everybody likes him. Do you think he'd do it?"

"I don't know. I've heard him tell people about the Lord, and he does a great job. He might."

"To start with, we could choose a short portion and help him study it," I said.

Dishes finished, we prayed about the decision and decided to talk with Felix the next day.

43

His answer was short and easy. "No! If I were to stand up to read," he said, "the words wouldn't rise as high as my throat." He stood up, grabbed his throat, and pretended to strangle on a few words. We laughed and tried to reassure him. He could not be persuaded; he was sure of the results.

We changed the subject. We both felt that Felix had a rare gift of sharing the gospel. We would be quiet and trust the Lord to lead him.

A week later we put the final polish on Mark before turning it in for publication. That evening, after an especially good session with Rosendo, Juan, and Aureliano present to "help" Felix, Felix's heart seemed touched by the account of the disciples struggling alone in their boat and Christ walking on the water to go to them.

When we finished the revision, Felix sat quietly rereading the carbon copy with its corrections, holding the paper at an odd angle to catch the lamplight. Without realizing what the result might be, I asked if he would like to stand closer to the lamp and read it aloud. He did so without a thought. As he sat down, his eye caught mine and I saw the twinkle that said, "Oh, oh! I just blew my theory about standing up and reading aloud."

Felix stalled a bit by the door as the others, one by one, said good-bye. Finally, he stood alone and looked up as if commenting on the millions of twinkling stars overhead. "You help me and I'll do it," he said.

Vi and I both knew what he meant. The Lord was preparing a Tila pastor even before they had a church!

5
"The Black Tortilla Talks"

The room was packed. Tilas crowded around the house, vying for space to get their heads in an open door or window to see the tall white man who had just gotten off the MAF plane. The lucky ones were close enough to reach out and touch him.

He opened a green wooden box and carefully placed something that looked like a black tortilla on a little round disk in the box. Then he motioned for Margarito, who somehow always managed to be in the center of everything, to crank the metal handle on the side of the box.

Margarito lowered his head and giggled shyly. He stepped forward; he wouldn't miss a chance for some new excitement. He cranked the handle and the crowd, as one person, gasped in fear and tried to step back. The "black tortilla" talked Spanish!

Jim Mittlestedt from Gospel Recordings had come to Chivalito to make a set of gospel records in the Tila language. The Tilas were thrilled when we explained that Jim had brought a battery-operated tape recorder that could "grab their words." Then he would record those words and make records in Tila just like the Spanish one he had just demonstrated. "In that way, Tilas in faraway villages can simply crank a handle as Margarito is doing and hear God's Word speak in the 'straight language,'" Vi explained.

Apprehension disappeared. The men almost smothered Jim as they surged around in an attempt to get a closer look at the marvelous little box.

Jim picked up a record and passed it to the tall, smiling Venancio, who had pushed his way to the front of the group. Venancio reached out to receive it, then hesitated, and jerked his hand back. His smile suddenly disappeared. What made that thing talk? Did he dare take it?

A rash of taunting giggles from the crowd embarrassed him. He bolstered his courage and reached for the record. When Venancio had it safely in hand, others eagerly reached out to touch it.

"Hey, it's hard," they called to those craning to get a glimpse of it.

"And it has tiny lines that go around and around it," Venancio observed.

They passed the record from one to another. As they examined it, they barraged us with questions that we passed on to Jim in English.

"Where are the words?"

"Why can't we see them like we see words on paper?"

"How do the words jump from this thing and speak with a voice like a person?"

Jim looked baffled, and I knew his mind was spinning in an effort to give a simple explanation.

Before Jim could speak, old Jorge's deep voice came from the back of the crowd. "It's the way God works," he said. "There's nothing too hard for God to do. He can make words jump from that black thing to the ears of people. He can do it because he wants people to hear the true words."

All was quiet. For a moment no one moved or spoke. In their minds, Jorge, a respected old man who had asked God to "turn his heart to the straight path" certainly had the right answer.

I translated Jorge's answer to Jim, and he nodded. The crowd was satisfied. No further explanation was needed.

The next three days sped by as we prepared, timed, checked, and rechecked scripts. School was dismissed so that Tila believers could meet in every available corner to study their scripts or practice special music. We had translated almost half of the New Testament, and many of the forty or so Chivalito Christians read well. Over the past two years, Vi had trained several singing groups. All were on hand to share the excitement and help in any way they could.

The school children also helped by shooing chickens and dogs away from our house, where Jim was "grabbing words." Visitors who came for medicine were stopped at a safe distance until I waved from our door to indicate that the word-grabbing machine had been turned off.

When visitors entered, Jim delighted in replaying the tape and watching their dark eyes widen as an awed expression slowly spread over their faces.

A week later the Tilas crowded into our yard as the MAF plane returned to Chivalito. All wanted to shake Jim's hand and say good-bye.

"You all did a fine job. This is excellent material," Jim said as he boarded the plane. "It'll take about four months to press the eight records and make copies." Referring to a note in his pocket, he added, "As soon as they're ready, I'll send you ten phonographs and fifty copies of each record."

"All clear," Gene, the pilot, called as he gave a final wave and closed the plane's window. The Tilas waved as the "metal bird" roared off the short, grassy strip.

Our lives returned to normal.

Teaching school still occupied much of our day but paid big dividends. Many older people accepted the Lord and were delighted to have children or grandchildren read to

47

them as they gathered around the open, flickering fires in their little pole-walled homes.

Margarito advanced to the third and then the fourth grade, always at the top of his class. Santiago was proud of his son, who not only "knew paper" but did equally well in writing, math, and Spanish.

A Saturday morning Bible club for all school-aged children became very popular. The children memorized Scripture verses and learned new hymns. Adults, too shy to sing in church, learned hymns at home. The jungle began to sing!

One day Amado, an illiterate witch doctor, came for medicine. While waiting, he walked over and stood gazing at a bulletin board on the clinic wall. He quietly studied every detail of an illustrated tract about heaven. Several Scripture verses typed on heavy construction paper caught his attention. These were like the cards his nine-year-old Lupita brought home from Bible club each week. Running his calloused fingers, word by word, over one of the cards, he repeated the verse as if he were reading it. *"Mach'an yambu ba' ch'ujbi lac tyaj laj cotyuntyel. Dios ma' ti yuc'onla yambu ti pejtyelel mulawil ba' mi lac tyaje' laj cotyuntyel. Cojach ti Jesus"* (Acts 4:12).

I looked up, startled. How had Amado learned to read? I turned away quickly when I realized that the verse he was saying was not the one he was fingering. He was running his fingers over that week's verse but saying last week's! The words of the verse, repeated by Lupita as she memorized them, had sunk into Amado's liquor-soaked brain. Would those words, by God's grace, ever change his hard heart?

We packed each day with ever-increasing activity. Our fifth anniversary in Chivalito came and went without any celebration.

A month later, at the regular 7:30 A.M. MAF communication, Gene announced that he had received several large cartons for us. "They are from the Publications Department," he said.

"Great," I exclaimed. "When can you arrange a flight?"

"How's Wednesday?" he asked.

"Super. We'll be waiting!"

The "jungle grapevine" spread the news: 1 and 2 Corinthians was published and would arrive on Wednesday.

The Christians planned a fiesta. Women and girls spent hours picking and toasting coffee; men made extra trips to the field to carry corn, which the women made into tamales; boys vied with each other to see who could carry the biggest load of firewood. Excitement reigned. More of God's Word was on the way!

After the celebration, attendance at the Bible study soared. The people now owned copies of Mark, Acts, 1 and 2 Thessalonians, 1 and 2 Timothy, Titus, and a brand new, light blue book—1 and 2 Corinthians. "We are rich," they said with a deep, satisfied sigh. "God speaks to us in Tila!"

Four months after Jim recorded the Tila messages, the roar of the MAF plane interrupted our math class. "Here it comes!" the children shouted. "See! There it is, coming through the pass."

The plane rumbled to a halt, and Gene unloaded the very special cargo—ten Gospel Recordings phonographs and several boxes of the long-awaited Tila records.

Most of the schoolchildren had not seen Jim's demonstration of a Spanish record and knew nothing of the project. We opened the boxes. The children crowded around as we placed a Tila record on one of the little phonographs. Margarito stepped up to crank the handle. The children

49

screamed and scrambled away as the words poured out of the new machine. "Look at it. It's alive!" they cried.

"The tortilla talks! The black tortilla talks," they shrieked.

Margarito, with a know-it-all air, explained about records. No class we had ever taught held their attention as did the messages cranked out of that little wooden box.

What began as a tiny trickle soon became a stream of requests from faraway villages. All wanted to hear the "black tortillas that talk." The next MAF flight brought twenty more of the popular little machines.

As we loaned each machine, we carefully wrote down the borrower's name and village. Since it was deemed very serious to have one's name marked on paper, almost all the phonographs were returned in good condition.

Felix and Aureliano, each with a traveling companion, spent about half their time visiting villages where people expressed interest in the gospel. Many villages, however, were so far away that they had never once heard the message of Jesus.

Domingo, a recently converted witch doctor, had once lived in such a village. In his mid-fifties, he was illiterate. His face was such a sea of wrinkles that they folded into each other and almost hid deep scars from machete cuts he had received in a drunken fight nearly fifteen years before. He fled his village after that fight and had never returned. But now things were different. Christ had "turned his heart around." His every waking thought was for his witch-doctor friends back in Torro. He wanted to tell them about the Lord.

Early one morning, Domingo swung one of the phonographs onto his back and secured it with a two-inch-wide strip of bark across his forehead. A small woven bag slung across his shoulder held the records, a gourd cup, and a large ball of cooked, ground corn wrapped in a banana leaf. Picking up his machete, he left for the two-day trip to Torro.

Domingo's friends greeted him warmly. They talked, laughed, and reminisced about the "old days." When they brought out a bottle of liquor, Domingo turned away and opened the phonograph. He put on a record and cranked the handle. The record spoke Tila and told of the living God who made the sun and moon that the Tilas worshiped as gods. Awed, they listened to several more records.

As the messages unfolded, Domingo explained that the God of the records had also turned his heart around; that he, too, had become a follower of the Savior.

At first, the friends were angry and incredulous.

"How can you, who have experienced the power and authority of a witch doctor, turn your back on the very gods who have chosen you?" one shouted. "Have you no pride? Have you no convictions?"

One bleary-eyed friend, sticking his face within inches of Domingo's, demanded, "Are you going to allow your life to become as useless as a woman's?"

Domingo did not become angry. Instead, he quietly told them about Christ, who had changed his life. He explained that Christ, who is the Son of God, made blind men see. He raised the dead. Surely the Christ he now followed had more power than their witchcraft. "My Christ is mighty enough to take the kind of stones we used in witchcraft and turn them into bread!" he explained.

He assured his friends that the messages they heard on the phonograph were really true. "I have believed in that Christ. He has made my heart feel good—good like nothing else I have ever experienced. You, too, should consider such a change. God will make your hearts tender toward him if you will ask him."

Domingo's friends couldn't understand how he could answer their shouts so quietly and calmly. That was not like the Domingo they remembered. They felt angry and betrayed.

"You have turned your back on the only true way," one of them screamed. With a furious wave of his hand, he ordered Domingo to leave Torro. "We never want to see you again," he shouted.

Domingo tried to plead with his friends. "No! Wait! There is another record that you must hear—just one more. God will make his message clear."

Instead, his friends grabbed their machetes and ordered him to leave. "Go now or we will show you how a real man uses a machete," they threatened.

Domingo hastily closed the phonograph and slipped the records into his carrying bag. Swinging the machine to his back, he started down the trail. He knew his friends well enough to realize that their threats were not idle words. But they hadn't understood the love of God. He *must* try just one more time to make it clear to them. He had to make them understand God's great love that had so completely conquered his heart. A few steps down the trail, he turned to make one last effort to share the gospel message with them. Furious, one of the men dashed down the trail after Domingo. His machete flashed and came down with a dull crunch on the phonograph slung across Domingo's back. Domingo's hand, resting on the machine to steady it, was in the path of the blade. As Domingo pulled his hand away, three fingers dropped on the grassy trail.

His anger vented, the man sheathed his machete and returned to his friends. Domingo hurried around a bend, then stepped off the trail. He tore a sleeve from his shirt and tightly bandaged his hand. He trudged wearily home.

Two days later as I dressed the stumps, Domingo reluctantly told me all that had happened. After a long pause, his quiet old eyes looked to mine and he said, "Those poor men! God's message just didn't grab their hearts. I'll go back and tell them again!"

I studied his face for a minute and then looked away. The wrinkles were there. The old scars were there. But there was also something else. In his eyes I could see a very deep and tender love for the Lord.

Long after the lights were out that night, I lay staring into the dark and thinking of Domingo's crippled hand. His quiet words, "I'll go back and tell them again," drummed in my ears.

I thought of the times I had failed to witness to my friends; of the times I resisted "going back and telling them again" when they had shown little interest in the gospel. I felt tears slip down my cheeks and dampen my pillow. I felt as if I were a failure. Though threatened with death, Domingo eagerly sought to do the very thing from which I had shrunk.

I turned over, struggled to my knees in the cramped confines under my mosquito net, and rededicated my life to the Lord. I asked him to make me as faithful a missionary as this humble, illiterate former witch doctor.

6
Not One Nail Hole

Every mosquito within miles must have been aware of the movable feast trudging along the slippery, muddy trail. A generous application of thick, oily mosquito repellent hadn't fazed them. They'd even discovered the inside of my ears. A few buzzed angrily as they became entangled in the short curly hair clinging to my damp forehead.

But today it would take more than hordes of mosquitoes to dampen our enthusiasm. Vi and I were on our way to see the church—the very first Tila church! Since the trail was new to us, we slowly picked our way along. Around a sharp bend, the trail narrowed and became choked with vines and thick jungle growth. After the recent heavy rains, it had turned into an ankle-deep quagmire of oozy, gooey mud.

Vi and I had just returned from a busy six-month mini-furlough, and it would take a few days to get used to jungle life again. I glanced down at my new blue and white high-topped tennis shoes. Why did I ever choose white? They looked nice in the store, but that bright clean store now seemed part of a completely different world.

Suddenly, from around the next bend, we heard Felix's voice, followed by the laughter of a large group of men. The sound of their voices encouraged us. We knew we were close. In spite of the mud and mosquitoes, we realized that this was our world.

We picked our way around one more long, lazy curve of the impossible trail and stepped into a clearing. The trip was worth every difficult step.

Before we had left for furlough, the men pointed out a hilltop field they were clearing. "We've decided to work together every Thursday," Felix said, "In March we'll plant beans. It'll be a big field. Maybe when we harvest it, there'll be enough money to buy galvanized metal for the church roof."

"Daddy says it needs metal because it is God's house and God deserves the best," piped up five-year-old Rosa.

Felix smiled and nodded. Santiago patted his daughter on the head and gently told her to shhh.

The men worked together well. When harvest time arrived, the women and children joined in the project. The Lord gave a good harvest—better than their individual fields. They smiled knowingly. "He is the One-whose-power-cannot-be-measured. He can do anything," they said to each other. They set aside the harvest money.

Weeks passed as they cut poles and prepared building materials. They prayed together and with real joy watched the project take shape. The villagers watched too, sure that sooner or later, the men would have a sharp disagreement. Experience told them that such projects usually ended in a free-for-all machete fight.

But no fight occurred. The villagers marveled. What could be so different about this group of people? They seemed to enjoy working together.

When the weather cleared and the trails dried, the men made the arduous two-day trip over the mountains to Macuspana to buy galvanized metal. Most had never been there before, but there would be no problem. Santiago, a vivacious member of the group, knew the way and would help with the purchases.

The bright sunny day matched their mood. They laughed and called to each other as they trekked along the narrow trail. "Our metal roof will wink at the sky," Andres laughed.

"Yes, maybe it'll even wink at the sun god," Venancio joked.

The men spent little time gaping at the sights in Macuspana. They made their purchase and left for home. Eighteen men made a long, curious looking column as they trudged along the trail, each with two sheets of metal rolled together and tied to his back.

With all the necessary building materials on hand, the superstructure went up quickly. When it was time to put on the roof, however, they were baffled. How does one put up a metal roof? No one knew. All their homes had thatch roofs.

Felix owned a hammer. Santiago borrowed one from a friend in Salto. Together they climbed to the peak of the church. Assembly-line fashion, tall Venancio handed two sheets of metal to Andres who passed them up to Santiago. He and Felix lapped the edge of one over the other, picked up the lead-top nail, then looked helplessly at each other. When up on top, how did one know where the rafter was? They considered their dilemma for a few minutes, then lowered the metal sheets and climbed down. The entire group stood together in the roofless building to think about the problem. They had not even come near our house those years before when the Tumbala Christians struggled with the metal roof. The Tumbala Christians had driven nails hither and yon seeking out the rafters that were "hidden" under the sheets of metal. Our roof was a huge galvanized metal sieve. There must be a better way.

Felix's sharp mind recalled a verse that he had helped us translate. He quoted it and reminded the men that God promised wisdom to those who asked. They knew God kept his promises. They bowed their heads and asked him to help them put up the roof—without nail holes.

Felix again picked up his hammer and climbed to the peak. Santiago climbed along at eave's level, squinted down each rafter and directed Felix's nail to find its exact mark in the crooked rafters.

As Felix told us the story, his eyes slowly roved over the beautiful roof twinkling in the afternoon sun. "This is the Lord's house, and we wanted it to be nice. He showed us how to put on the roof without one nail hole in it," Felix said reverently.

Vi and I watched for a few minutes as work continued. The dull red, ironwood corner posts looked as if they would last forever. Aureliano and Valerio, soaked with perspiration, carefully measured and cut round balsa poles. Juan and Candelario lashed them in place in an upright position to form walls. "Surely the Lord must be pleased with the work of those men whose changed lives reflect their love for him," Vi said.

We forgot the buzzing mosquitoes and our muddy feet as we stood under the unusual roof of the almost-completed church. Vaguely aware of the animated conversation around me, I stared at the roof. I knew the Chivalito Christians would face other problems in the future, but when they did, they would have a Book in their hands—a Book filled with God's promises, promises like the one they had claimed as they struggled to erect a metal roof, a roof without one nail hole.

7
"The Owl Killed My Baby"

"Show me how to make bubbles. Here's my gum. Show me how."

I had buried my nose in a desk full of reference books, trying to ferret out the meaning of the fifth chapter of Romans and was only half aware of Pedro's incessant demand. When he stuck his two-day-old piece of bubble gum up to my lips, I dropped my pen and focused on Pedro and his "need" to blow bubbles.

Six-year-old Pedro lived next door and was among the youngsters always vying to wash our muddy tennis shoes in a nearby stream. A piece of bubble gum was a small price to pay for clean shoes or a host of other child-sized jobs.

"See. I blow, but I can't make it puff" he explained, as he puckered up his little lips in an exaggerated effort to produce a bubble. He laid one hand across my book as if to flash a stop sign, then with the other hand quickly took the gum from his mouth and held it up to my face. "Here. You try," he said.

"That's OK, Pedro. You keep it. You'll need it in order to practice. I'll get another piece," I responded, as I stepped to the jar containing our supply. Then, trying to forget the translation, I settled down to chew and teach. Pedro was an apt pupil. After a few demonstrations, he blew a large round bubble that exploded on his lips with a soft puff. His eyes twinkled with a thousand tiny stars as he picked the gum off his lips, shoved it back into his mouth, and repeated the performance. Then, without a word, he dashed out the door to show off his great accomplishment of the day. With a sigh, I got back to Romans.

Before the chapter was finally captured on paper, four-year-old Marta flitted through the door, stuck her head under my elbow, and snuggled up to the translation desk. Handing me the *Reader's Digest*, she looked up into my face and said, "Let's sing."

I pushed my chair back and she crawled up onto my lap. "Let's sing this one," she said, putting her chubby little finger on a page of the upside down book. Since the *Digest* didn't afford much of a clue as to what she wanted to sing, I gave her a light kiss on the forehead and said, "OK, you start it." She complied and started in the middle of "Trust and Obey." We finished that hymn and sang two more that I had often heard Marta and her parents sing at family devotions. But I couldn't sing all day. Romans was waiting! I gave her a gentle shove off my lap. She fixed her big brown eyes on me and said, "At home we always pray after we sing!" We prayed. After Marta left, I sat for several minutes trying to recapture my train of thought and continue the verse. I picked up my pen and started writing.

A babble of voices cut though my concentration, excited voices—voices of people carrying someone. "Ruby, are you here?" they shouted. "Jeronimo's badly hurt."

By the time I sutured and bandaged the five-inch machete wound, it was too late to go back to my desk. Romans would wait another day. I was discouraged and frustrated.

It was urgent that we complete the translation. But many things—classes for children and adults, medical work, Bible clubs, and women's Bible studies—these all cut into translation time. We stayed up later at night and got up earlier in the morning, but translation goals continually eluded us.

One evening, after a particularly frustrating day in which neither of as came close to our goals, Vi and I decided to make some major changes in our schedule. We felt trapped. We needed to make time for the Christians so they could grow. But making time for them thwarted progress in Bible translation—our main reason for being here. We stood in the open door, soaked up the coolness of the night and watched the moon slip from behind a hill and slide into the night sky. We were too discouraged to feel sleepy. We needed to reset goals, rearrange schedules...but how?

"What we need is a solid, uninterrupted block of time. Just grabbing an hour here and there isn't working for me," Vi said.

I know," I replied. "Mornings are a washout for me, too. By the time I really get into a passage, it's time for school to start."

The bright moon cast shadows that looked like midday. The scent of a variety of jungle flowers permeated the cool breeze. We sighed, picked up our folding chairs, and moved to the yard. We had to think. We had to find a way to make progress on the translation. But what could we omit? Everything we were doing was important to the growth of the church. But without God's Word in their hands, that growth would be stunted.

The moon continued to inch its way across the sky as we discussed one idea after another and abandoned each in turn. After a long pause in which neither of us spoke, Vi said, "What do you think would happen, if instead of translating for an hour and a half each morning before school, we just started school at 6:30 instead of 8:00 A.M. If we did that for four days a week, we would be adding six hours to the school schedule. Then on Friday we could dismiss the children altogether. That way, they would have all morning free to either go to the field or stay with the little ones so their mothers could go."

Vi had spoken slowly, thinking things out as she went along. By the time she finished, the idea was full-grown in my mind. Smiling, we finished the last sentence in unison, "And we would have all morning free to translate!"

The more we talked about it, the better we liked the idea. An hour later, with the moon high in the sky, we bowed our heads and thanked the Lord for a plan we felt was his answer to our dilemma.

The next day we talked with parents. They were enthusiastic. The women considered it such a great idea that they wanted to extend it to their classes as well. We happily stretched their hours a bit each day and dismissed their Friday class.

The church family was large by now, and many people clamored for a tiny piece of our time. That Sunday, Pastor Felix talked about the urgency of the translation project and our need for uninterrupted study time. The congregation agreed that, although there would be no school on Friday, no one should visit us on that day. Only emergencies would be treated in the clinic. The entire day was dedicated to translation.

Word soon spread to the surrounding villages that Ruby and Vi didn't "work" on Fridays. They just "sat and stared at paper." Most people, however, cooperated, and we made good progress on the translation.

We spent Friday mornings in study and preparation of a rough draft of that day's portion. Felix and Aureliano, usually accompanied by several others, spent the late afternoons and evenings helping us make it speak good Tila.

As we translated, Felix often became so thrilled with the message, that he copied verses to take home and share with

Petrona. He memorized many verses and sprinkled them throughout his sermons.

Margarito, now thirteen and an excellent reader, spent hours proofreading the typed manuscript. Chapter after chapter, book after book, the translation progressed. Finally, the end was in sight. The Tila New Testament would soon become a book.

The church also progressed. Felix, Rosendo, Juan, and Aureliano had all become good preachers. But these four also enjoyed evangelizing and were often gone from the village on Sunday. The solution was obvious: we would train more preachers, teachers, and evangelists.

We began a "preacher-training" class with eight promising young men. After several weeks of study, the time came for each, in turn, to preach to his peers in class, followed by the even more difficult task of criticizing each other's presentation.

Arturo, Rosendo's son-in-law, a bright, studious young man, was shy and wanted to be last.

When Arturo's turn came, we sat in stunned silence. As his message unfolded, it was excellent. The only criticism anyone could have offered (but didn't) was that his bare toes almost dug a hole to China in the soft dirt floor.

After conducting a home Bible study a few times and taking charge of the Wednesday prayer meeting, Arturo lost his shyness and became an excellent preacher with a deep, sincere love for God's Word.

Arturo's wife, Adela, a pretty young lady with twinkling eyes and a pleasant smile, shared his new ministry. Years before, Adela had been one of the first girls allowed to attend school. Now an excellent reader, she and Arturo studied the Bible together.

Before Arturo and Adela accepted the Lord, they had had two children, both of whom died in infancy. About a year after they became Christians, little David was born. He was a beautiful baby, and Adela referred to him as her "little preacher boy."

One evening when David was about a month old, Vi and I visited the young couple and took the baby a gift. He cooed and blew tiny bubbles and was the center of attention.

That night I awakened and heard an owl hooting in the distance. I lay still, thinking about Tila superstitions and their awful fear of the owl, "the-bird-that-steals-spirits."

After a few minutes, the hooting stopped. I was almost asleep when I heard running feet approaching our house. I jumped out of bed as Arturo reached our door. His eyes were big, and his tongue stumbled on his words. "Ruby, it's the owl. It got in. I tried to drive it away, but I couldn't. It flew in and snatched David's spirit. Little David is dead."

Rosendo and his wife and a few close neighbors were at Arturo's home when we arrived. All were telling him that if he had kept the owl out, this would not have happened.

What could we say? Everyone fully believed the owl was responsible for David's sudden death. One after another, they repeated stories—stories of the bird and its cruel attacks.

Adela sat in a dim corner, holding her dead baby and quietly sobbing. Arturo, his head in his hands, was over-whelmed and bewildered. He had tried to keep the owl out. He had batted it with cornhusks. After several attempts, however, the owl slipped past his flailing arms. His eyes searched his father-in-law's for understanding. Rosendo nodded sympathetically.

Vi and I looked into the faces of our friends. Everyone in the room feared the owl with a deep and dreadful fear. Everyone believed the owl stole human spirits—had believed it all their lives. To them, David's death was further evidence!

How could we tell these people that the owl couldn't snatch spirits? They would listen; they would know we wanted to help—but they would believe that we, as outsiders, didn't *really* understand about the owl.

We sat and prayed—prayed for wisdom and for understanding hearts. To us, the owl's power was not real; it was superstition. To these people, it was true and deadly.

The funeral was difficult as unasked questions often trembled on Adela's lips. "If the owl is the symbol of the devil, where was God? Isn't God stronger than the devil?"

During the next few days, Vi and I prayed for them, suffered with them, and spoke when we could. We read translated portions of Scripture to them and spontaneously translated other portions. We longed for the day when the whole New Testament would be in their hands.

The church family also stood by. They prepared meals, read Scripture with Arturo and Adela, and prayed with them.

Many of Arturo's friends, disturbed by his stand for the Lord, wasted no time in pointing out all the reasons why he should turn his back on his new religion. In their minds this was further evidence that God wasn't really the Almighty One as Arturo claimed.

An almost visible tug of war surged in Arturo's and Adela's hearts. We prayed that the superstitions and beliefs they had inherited from their parents, grandparents, and great-grandparents wouldn't overwhelm their new belief in God.

After days of quiet struggle and doubt, Arturo asked the questions that plagued them: "If God is really God, why didn't he stop the owl from coming into our house? If God is loving and almighty, why did he allow the owl to kill

David?" We welcomed the questions and prayerfully answered them from God's Word.

Two hours later, tears in their eyes, Arturo and Adela quietly acknowledged that the Lord is the only one who can give or take life. They didn't understand, but surely God did. They would trust Him.

With a new tenderness in his voice, Arturo preached a number of messages on heaven. The gospel had won another victory!

Tila Christians continued to evangelize—now reaching eighteen villages. The ever-popular Gospel Recordings phonographs faithfully cranked out their messages to dozens of wide-eyed family gatherings in new areas. The gospel spread; lives changed.

In spite of these things, however, I often lay awake at night thinking about almost two hundred widely scattered Tila villages where people still had not heard of God's love. Was there some other way of getting that message to them? During the long nights, I often meditated on many God-given promises. Almost always my heart came back to 2 Peter 3:9, which assured me that "The Lord ... is not willing that any should perish, but that all should come to repentance." There had to be a way—a faster way—to get that message across mile after mile of trackless jungle.

8
Tila Radio Programs

Luis, the leader of the "jet set" in Chivalito, was the first to own a battery-operated transistor radio. No one understood Spanish, but that didn't matter. At any time of the day or night, a twist of a knob produced loud, jazzy marimba or guitar music. The wilder and louder the music, the better everyone enjoyed it. A crowd always gathered to listen and mimic. Children soon reeled off advertising slogans in Spanish with no idea of what they said.

On my first visit to Luis's house after he proudly installed his radio on its own balsa pole shelf, I felt as if my eyes were in one century, and my ears in another! How incredible to listen to a modern radio while sitting on a balsa log in a one-room, dirt-floor, thatched-roof hut, where the only dishes were either gourds or homemade clay bowls. Incredible or not, the fad soon swept the Tila area. Tilas, struggling under the weight of an eighty-pound bag of coffee trudged over the steep mountainous trail to Salto, eager to exchange their load for a radio and a box of batteries. Soon almost half of the Tila households in Chivalito owned one of the prestigious little instruments.

Luis's house was close to ours, which meant that at four-thirty every morning his radio became our alarm. One morning in the predawn darkness, my sleepy brain registered that the "noise" had been replaced by a hymn. When the music ended, Luis quickly turned to another station. He made no effort to listen to the message for he understood only Tila.

I sat up in bed, my mind a jumble of thoughts. Would it be possible to broadcast the gospel in an Indian language?

How could we find out? Was there a Mexican law to forbid it? Would the Tilas be able to produce such a program'?

I lay down and closed my eyes, remembering the excellent message Arturo had preached on Sunday. I longed for thousands to be able to hear such messages. Quite possibly there were laws against a broadcast in an Indian language. But God is Almighty; if he wanted the Tilas to hear his message by radio, no law could prevent it.

I listened to Luis's jabbering "box" and visualized isolated Tila huts with people clustered around a radio listening to Arturo's message. I remembered the role that radio had in my salvation. I grew up in Palatka, Florida, with a Catholic mother and a non-Catholic father. My parents dearly loved each other; so to avoid possible conflict, they agreed not to go to either church. Religion was not mentioned.

When I entered first grade, my teacher asked if I went to Sunday school. I didn't understand the question.

"Sunday school?" I asked, parroting her intonation. "I didn't know I was supposed to come to school on Sunday. My big brother comes to your school, and he only comes on Monday, Tuesday, Wednesday, Thursday, and Friday," I said slowly, hoping to impress her with my knowledge of the days of the week.

She smiled, gave me a Gideon New Testament, and told me about the Lord.

I loved school with its wide halls and low, white drinking fountains that squirted ice water in my face and hair. "School is going to be fun," I thought, as I dashed home to show mother my beautiful white book with its shiny gold letters.

"Look, Mom. Miss Menton gave me a gift. Will you read it to me?"

A dark sidelong glance warned me not to pursue the subject. "Mom is busy," I thought. "I'll wait until evening when she sits down to read."

That evening I again handed her my book. "Here, Mom, will you read to me now?"

"No," she said sharply. "Put that book away. I don't ever want to see it again."

Puzzled, I put it away. "That's OK." I thought to myself. "Daddy will be home tomorrow. He'll read to me."

The next day I met Dad as the car pulled into the circular drive. I gave him a big hug and held up my new book. "Look what Miss Menton gave me," I said, proudly pointing to the gold letters. "Will you read to me, Daddy?"

An hour later I snuggled onto Dad's lap as he opened the book and examined it. I didn't understand the faraway look in his eyes as he slowly thumbed through several pages. I patiently waited for him to find a "story" and read.

Finally he gave me a little hug and said, "Honey, your new book is beautiful, but it has lots of things in it that a little girl your age doesn't need to know. Go put it away, and don't think about it any more. Bring me another book, and we'll read a little while."

He looked at the New Testament another minute, closed it, and gently pushed me off his lap.

That settled it. Daddy always knew best, and he said I didn't need to worry about what was in that book. And Mom didn't want to read it either. I happily scampered to my room, put my book away, and climbed back onto Daddy's lap with another one.

The Lord, however, had a specific plan for my life—a plan that involved the New Testament.

Each day of my first six years in grade school was started with Scripture reading and the Lord's Prayer—and each day I became hungrier for God's Word.

After I learned to read, I memorized many verses from my hidden New Testament. From friends I learned about Sunday school but was never allowed to go. I was also forbidden to listen to Christian radio programs.

During my freshman year in high school, although my parents forbade it, I secretively listened to a program. The pastor quoted many of the verses I had memorized. They spoke to my heart, and for the first time, I understood the gospel. As the program closed, I knelt beside the radio and accepted the Lord.

The radio! What a marvelous instrument for taking God's Word to hungry hearts in hidden places. Surely the Almighty God could slice through the most insurmountable obstacles so that radios could get that same message to the Tilas. There must be a way. I would start work on it that very day.

Henry and Charlene Stegenga, administrators of a fine three-year Bible School in the Tumbala dialect, had lived among the Tumbalas for fifteen years. Hank's easygoing manner, quick wit, and beautiful way with words—Spanish, Tumbala, or English—won many friends in all three cultures. He would know whom to contact to answer the myriad questions tugging at my brain.

The Stegengas had recently visited us and were thrilled with what the Lord was doing among the Tilas.

They had warmly invited us to spend some weekend with them. This would be a good time. Although their village was several days away by trail, the MAF plane could lift us above the swift rivers and steaming jungle. We radioed MAF on our daily contact and made arrangements for the fifteen-minute flight.

Sitting on the Stegengas' wide, screened porch and sipping cold lemonade, we told them of the fad sweeping the Tila area. I poured out my impossible-sounding dream of the radio reaching thousands of Tilas with the gospel.

"Hey, you know, I think you really have something there," Hank said with a wide grin. "When I was in Salto last month, Alfredo's Mercantile was selling radios like hot cakes. He told me he had ordered six more cases."

"Yes, at first we thought they might just be in Chivalito," Vi said, "But Aureliano and Rosendo commented on how many there are in the Limar area."

"And Felix said they're as far south as Lumija. When he and Lindo passed through there Friday afternoon, they stopped and witnessed to nine men who were stretched out listening to a marimba band," I added with a laugh.

"We've heard of a few in the Tumbala area," Char said as she refilled our glasses. "Radios could provide a tremendous opportunity to share the gospel."

"That's right! But now we need to find a way to capitalize on them," I said, eager to get on with the "how-to" discussion.

"There must be a way," Hank said, staring into his glass, idly watching one lonely ice cube bump around.

Conversation slowed. We all recognized the potential, but how could we make it happen?

In the quietness I became aware of the rhythmic slap of water as a group of Tumbala Indians poled their canoe down the Tulija River that ran past Hank's home. They waved and called a greeting as the canoe rounded the bend and slipped from sight.

Hank sat stroking his chin, oblivious to the beads of perspiration that gathered at his hairline and trickled down his face.

"Do you know Ildefonso Pulido?" he asked with sudden inspiration.

"No. Who's he?"

"He's a Mexican pastor in Macuspana. About a year ago he told me that the town had recently built a radio station and asked him if he wanted a slot of time on Sunday afternoons. He's talked with me about his program a couple of times. Says it's going great. Perhaps he could pull some strings and get you on the air in Macuspana."

"Do you mean there's a radio station in Macuspana?" I asked raising my eyebrows. "I thought Macuspana was just a little 'one horse' town."

"It's pretty small, all right," Hank laughed, "but I guess the town leaders know how to get things done."

"You should see that radio tower," Char said, stretching her arm as high as she could reach. "Aside from a few stores, it's about the only thing there!"

"Yeah, and Ildefonso says it's working out well. He started with a thirty-minute program and had such a good response that the station increased his time to forty-five minutes."

"How powerful a station is it? Would it reach to our area?" Vi asked.

"Oh yeah, no problem. Ildefonso said he has had responses from people as far away as the Yucatan Peninsula," Hank answered.

"But we're still talking about programming in Spanish," I protested. "Airing a program in Tila may be a whole different ball game. After all, the owners of the station won't understand a word that is said. Would they dare allow it?"

Hank was thoughtful for a few minutes. "I doubt that that would be a problem if Ildefonso would be willing to take the responsibility of airing your program as part of his. He's lived there all his life. They know and respect him."

Hours later we agreed that when MAF came to take us back to Chivalito, Hank would ask them to drop him off in Macuspana so he could talk with Pastor Ildefonso.

"I think Ildefonso will help you," Char said. "We've visited him and his wife a few times. They have a deep interest in the Indians."

Ten-year-old Karl had joined us on the porch. "Hey, Dad, I think that'll be cool," he said with a laugh. "Just think— broadcasting the gospel to homes that don't have stoves or furniture or dishes. Nothing—just radios!"

The weekend sped by as we discussed program preparation, format, and content, as well as needed equipment. We also decided that since radios were finding their way to the Tumbala area, we would divide the work. The Tumbala Christians would prepare programs for the first two weeks of the month and the Tilas would take the last two.

Three weeks later a note from Hank confirmed Ildefonso's excitement at the prospect of sharing radio time with the Tumbala and Tila areas.

"Muy bien," he exclaimed. "I've taken care of arrangements here. I'd love to help the Indians have their own program."

Wanda McKeever Rankin and Ruby Hanson visited us a month later and brought a new battery-operated Uher tape recorder. Vi developed several singing groups. All were excited. We were on our way—or so we thought.

Message preparation was a major undertaking. In church, pastors always preached at least an hour, some longer. This was expected and appreciated since many people walked for several hours to attend services. They wanted to hear as much of God's Word as possible. How could we expect men who had never owned a watch or clock to suddenly be able to squeeze a hymn, message, and a prayer all into a fifteen-minute program?

After weeks of frustrating trial and error, we solved the dilemma by preparing, timing, and typing each message. The pastor practiced it to perfection. Then, with children posted in strategic places to delay approaching visitors, as well as to keep crowing roosters and barking dogs at a safe distance, the "word-grabbing machine" whirred into action and the message was recorded.

Recording hymns to precede or follow the message also proved a challenge. No amount of practice produced a singing group that could start in unison on the first word of a hymn. Tilas are great followers, and by the end of the first line, most of the singers had chimed in some place. By the second line they might even have gotten on the same pitch! The end of the verse always found them singing together and sounding great.

After much frustration, I discovered the recorder's pause button held the perfect answer. With the button in pause position, the group sang the first verse. By the end of the verse, all had chimed in and were singing in unison. I gave the pause button a quick flick as they continued the hymn—starting again on the first verse and continuing to the end. They sounded terrific! Hymns, including women's and children's singing groups, became an important part of the programs.

On an exciting and memorable day in December 1970, thousands of surprised people tucked away in tiny villages across a vast jungle area stared at little radios suddenly speaking Tila—the "straight language." People without radios gathered at the homes of friends and listened together.

The Spanish-speaking president of Salto took advantage of Tila programs to get some "straight words" to the prisoners in the local jail, most of whom were Indians. He boomed each program over the loudspeaker attached to the jail wall. Activity in the public square came to a standstill as Tilas, awed at hearing their language on the radio, gaped up at the speaker. In stunned silence they listened to the hymns and messages.

Although Tilas have no native songs, hymns attracted them. Often, as the traveling preacher and his walking companion passed through a village, a crowd gathered and asked the men to sing hymns they had heard on the radio. Since the hymns contained gospel messages, the men gladly complied.

Marcial, a member of the dreaded Cruz clan, was attracted to the gospel through hymns. Little six-year-old Timothy, Felix and Petrona's oldest son, often sang as he visited his uncle. Marcial enjoyed the hymns and attended services to hear more. Soon the Cruz hilltop resounded with song. Filemon, Marcial's brother, liked what he heard and accompanied him to church. Both accepted the Lord and began the exciting walk down the "straight path."

Marcial had a beautiful voice and soon became the leader of the congregational singing. At this point., the hymnal contained more than a hundred hymns, and the song service often lasted an hour or more. With the initiation of the radio ministry, we appointed Marcial to be in charge of that part of the programming.

After a few weeks of carefully writing out the messages, the preachers gauged time more accurately, and program preparation became easier. We often prepared several tapes in one evening.

Tilas, always fascinated with the tape recorder, gathered eagerly at my elbow as I opened the machine to change batteries. "That machine eats lots of batteries," they said with a smile and a wag of the head.

On many occasions people stopped by our house on their return from Salto, dug down into their load of supplies, and handed me a couple of batteries as a gift for the "word grabber."

Gospel radio programs made an impact. Eager to hear the message of love, more and more villages welcomed the evangelists. Several teams went out from Chivalito each weekend.

My dream had come true. The radio message that had changed my life as a teenager was now available to those of a different language and culture—a language and culture that had become mine by adoption.

9
The Witch Doctor's Threat

It all started with what sounded like an absurd childish brag. That brag, however, struck fear in many hearts. Lencho, reputed to be the most powerful witch doctor in the area, openly vowed to completely destroy the growing Christian testimony in Chivalito. He didn't say how or when, but he promised that it would be irreversibly complete.

Scripture memorization was an important part of the regular Sunday services, so for the next several weeks, we chose verses that emphasized the power and authority of God. In spite of assurances in the Word that Christ has power over the demon world, we realized that even we were waiting—waiting to see what Lencho would do. Waiting—and expecting something traumatic to happen to the believers.

Weeks slipped past and nothing happened. People relaxed a bit. But Lencho, an unscrupulous and crafty old man, was in no hurry to carry out his threat. He planned carefully.

Rosendo, the former village drunk, now a hardworking family man, loved and served the Lord. He was also president of the congregation. In addition, Rosendo had saved his money and bought one of the first horses ever owned in Chivalito. The horse was the center of attention as men gathered around its corral in the evening, watching its every move.

"Look at the way he swishes his bushy tail," Luis laughed. "He acts angry."

"His tail would make a nice broom for Petrona," Felix teased.

To get a better view, ten-year-old Tino climbed the corral and clutched the top rail. "Hey, look at his tail. It's got a piece of brush tangled in it," he shouted. "I'll go get it out."

"Don't you go in there," his father admonished. "He's got big teeth. How do we know whether or not horses bite?"

"Hey, he heard you say that!" Venancio laughed.

"Yeah, did you see how pointed his ears got when he looked at you?" Lindo chimed in.

The horse continued to look intently at the crowd for a long minute, then stamped his foot, put his head down, and continued munching grass. The crowd hooted with laughter. "He understands Tila," they shouted to each other.

One evening Lencho joined the group as they stood around admiring the horse. "I once worked for a man who owned a horse," he said. "Señor Jose, in Tabasco, taught me how to train a horse to carry loads. I'll be glad to help you with your horse, if you want me to."

Rosendo considered the offer and thought that it might be a good opportunity to establish better rapport with Lencho and have an effective witness to him. Rosendo decided that if Lencho mentioned it again, he would accept.

Lencho was back in a couple of days and repeated his offer. Rosendo sent the horse home with him that evening.

Two days later Lencho came to Rosendo's house, seemingly very upset, and reported that someone had come in the night and stolen the horse.

That began what turned into a long search that cost Rosendo hundreds of pesos and weeks of time out of his field. His friends urged him to give up the search and pointed out that he could buy another horse for less than he was spending looking for that one. Rosendo wanted his own horse back.

Late one afternoon Lencho visited Rosendo and reported that someone had seen the horse at a Mexican's ranch a day's walk away.

"Señor Lopez, a lawyer in Salto, can get your horse back if you'll pay him and provide his plane fare," Lencho promised.

Rosendo, grateful for what he thought was a friendly tip, paid Senor Lopez two hundred pesos and made the arrangements for a flight to the ranch.

The trap was set.

The rancher was a notorious drunk and close friend of the lawyer who also loved his bottle.

Rosendo found himself in a wild drinking spree with Mexicans, whom he considered his superiors. Hour after hour he refused to drink. But Rosendo's Spanish was very limited and, as the drinking continued, they became increasingly insistent that he join them. He couldn't find the way of escape!

Late Saturday afternoon when the plane returned to Salto, people stared as Rosendo, the president of the Tila congregation, stumbled from the plane drunk. Lencho was very pleased with the success of his plan.

As Rosendo staggered over the three-hour trail making his slow, miserable way back to Chivalito, the story of his condition arrived with record speed and many embellishments. By that evening the Chivalito Christians were the laughingstock of the village.

"So this is the way the 'new life' works," Jeronimo scoffed, accompanied by a roar of laughter from the crowd.

"Look at the 'singers' now. Maybe they know another song we haven't heard," someone jeered.

Laughing and slapping their thighs, another would add, "We should go to their meetings. Maybe they explain how they are going to get enough liquor to heaven to keep all of them happy."

The ridicule and taunting was merciless. Lencho was on hand to fan the fire. Sunday afternoon the Christians were in a somber mood as they gathered for a church service. All had been ridiculed and laughed at. Rosendo was not present.

A few hymns later, Rosendo stepped from the jungle path into the church clearing and made his way to the building. Eyes down, he walked in and took his seat on the front row. When the hymn ended, he indicated he wanted to speak.

He stood up, eyes on the ground, and in a clear, concise way told what had happened. He didn't minimize what he had done, nor did he make excuses for himself. When he finished, he quoted 1 John 1:9. "If we confess our sins, he is faithful and just to forgive us our sins, and to cleanse us from all unrighteousness." He said he had confessed his sin to the Lord and the Lord had forgiven him. His voice choked with emotion as he looked up at the congregation and said, "I have not only brought shame to our Lord, but to you, too. All of you have been ridiculed and taunted because of what I did. I'm sorry. I don't know if you want to forgive me or not." He sat down, his head in his hands.

Felix, who happened to be home that Sunday, stood and said, "Remember a few weeks ago when it rained for three days without letting up?"

I looked up, startled. Everyone's attention had been glued on Rosendo, and emotions were at a peak. Felix's comment seemed completely out of context. Why was Felix talking about the rain? Hadn't he been listening? Could he possibly have had his mind on something else while Rosendo spoke?

Then Felix continued, "That rain left a huge mud puddle in our front yard. Several times Elpidio (his three-year-old son) dashed out the door to play in the muddy water. 'Elpidio,' I called, 'get away from that mud.' But after several attempts, he finally made his way to the puddle. Suddenly I heard an awful SPLAT and a cry. Elpidio was face down in the mud.

"Now friends," Felix continued, "What do you think I said? Do you think I just stood there rubbing my hands together and said, 'Well, I told you. Now it's your problem!' No, of course not. Elpidio is my little son and I love him. I hurried to him, picked him up, wiped the mud from his face, and held him until he quit crying.

"Friends, our brother Rosendo has fallen on his face in the mud! We have a Heavenly Father who loves him, has helped him up, and wiped the mud off him. He will hold him close and love him until the pain and embarrassment goes away. All of us have felt the splat of Rosendo's fall. We have been laughed at—and it hurt. But our Lord suffered a much deeper hurt for the things we have done than we will ever suffer because of what Rosendo did. Rosendo has confessed his sin, and the Lord has forgiven him. Now he is asking us to forgive him too."

Felix paused for a long minute and looked around as if thinking about what to do. Then, in a quiet voice he said, "Let's take a vote. All who want to forgive Rosendo and pray for him, put up your hand."

The congregation had been quiet as Felix talked, and I was aware that several were making an occasional quick wipe at their eyes. As I also pushed back a tear, I momentarily thought of friends at home. What would they think of this service, and especially Felix's unusual proposal?

But this was not the United States. This was a completely different world! These Tila Christians were making a bold, unashamed move to show one of their own that, although they had been hurt by his actions, they understood and didn't condemn him. They loved him and would stand with him. Together, they would step around the mud hole and continue on the "straight path."

As the congregation voted, I sensed, more than heard, the hands go up. I glanced around. The room was a sea of hands. Felix stepped over and touched Rosendo's shoulder and whispered to him. Rosendo glanced around then buried his face in his hands. I knew he was deeply touched.

With no announcement, Marcial stood and his deep voice rang out with the first words of "How Great Thou Art." With one accord the congregation joined in, and the church rang with great swells of joy as the words of the hymn showered us with new meaning. That hymn was followed by another and another. The song service continued to rock the church for an hour before Felix stood up to preach.

Although I'm sure his sermon was spontaneous, it was the best I've ever heard. It dealt with grace and forgiveness and was tailored to fit the situation. I marveled again at the number of verses Felix quoted throughout his sermon—verses not yet in printed form—verses he had written on slips of paper as we translated them.

The service dismissed. I watched as one after another, the men who had come in with heads down, discouraged, and shaken, grasped Rosendo's hand and reaffirmed their promise to pray for one another. They went home with heads high and a song on their lips.

Lencho's plan had failed! Love had won a victory—love that could leap over hurt and taunting and ridicule; love that could forgive, even while pain was still strong; love that marked the whole congregation as disciples of Christ. "By

81

this shall all men know that ye are my disciples, if you have love one to another" (John 13:35).

Vi and I realized that day that the Word of God had not only been translated into the Tila language, but, more importantly, it had been translated into Tila hearts and had produced Christlike action.

To God be the glory!

10
"Let Me Off the Merry-Go-Round"

Vi and I had lived in Chivalito for almost ten years. Our friends teased that, although life in the jungle was "rustic," we at least avoided the "rat race" at home. But during the past year our jungle life had moved so fast that we felt as if we were on a huge merry-go-round and couldn't get off.

The villagers built two schools—both now crowded to capacity. Many people had turned to the Lord, and everyone wanted to read the Scripture. We published several books of the New Testament as separate portions for those eager to study God's Word.

Tilas in a number of outlying villages accepted the Lord as traveling preachers shared the gospel. They marveled at "marks on paper" and wanted to learn to read. We prepared small blackboards, flashcards, syllable charts, and teaching aids that the preachers included in their backpacks. As they shared the gospel, they also shared the wonders of "knowing paper." In each area there were many eager students—mostly young men.

Year after year the school in Chivalito progressed, and we added writing, math, Mexican history, and Spanish to the curriculum. Writing was a challenge since most people had never held a pencil—or even a fork or spoon. Soon, however, they conquered the "special stick" and were able to express themselves on paper.

From the beginning, Tilas loved math and quickly progressed from simple addition to complicated fractions. As the class advanced, Vi included problems in which they calculated the price they should receive for a load of coffee or corn. But in real experience, how could they know how much a load was worth unless they knew the exact weight of that load?

To show our appreciation to them for replacing our dirt floor with a cement one, we bought the village a large, commercial-type scale. They were pleased with their gift and excitedly agreed that the best place for it was on the new cement floor.

On market day, our home became a hubbub of activity as men gathered to weigh their loads before making the slow, arduous trip to Salto.

To their surprise and chagrin, Salto merchants soon discovered that many Tilas had learned to calculate the price of their goods. Any unscrupulous merchant who was tempted to cheat had second thoughts as the Tilas pulled out a pencil, did some quick calculations, and told the prospective buyer exactly how much he expected for his load.

Spanish remained the most popular subject in school, and as the people became more fluent, the outside world seemed to open a crack.

A fellow translator published a series of agricultural books in simple Spanish. Tila readers enjoyed them and plagued us with questions about terracing, fertilizing, and pesticides. Since neither of us knew the answers, we invited the author, David Jarvis, to visit Chivalito. Three weeks later, Dave and son-in-law, Bob Short, arrived with more books, seed packs, and an array of equipment.

Both Dave and Bob were from England but had spent many years in Mexico and spoke Spanish fluently. They appreciated Indians and were tireless workers. For two weeks they answered questions and taught the men to terrace the hillsides. They also helped them plant small vegetable gardens close to their homes. We were happy with the results but even more delighted to see Tilas leap a great language barrier and communicate in Spanish. The door to the outside world opened a bit wider.

As the men lost their reticence to speak Spanish, we felt it was time for another step. All their lives they had relied on open water holes. Those holes dried up in the hot season and became horrible pits of contamination in rainy season as village waste washed into them. We explained wells and pumps and how they worked. The villagers were enthusiastic. With their encouragement, we invited a team of Spanish-speaking technicians to Chivalito to direct the men as they dug a large well, cemented it in, and installed a water tower and pump. They also placed a drinking fountain beside the schools. The days of open, contaminated water holes were past.

During our first two years in Chivalito, although I am an R.N., medical work had been exempt from the ever-increasing speed of the merry-go-round. There had been three witch doctors in the village. No one had had any interest in "outside" medicine.

During those years, Vi and I often shuddered and prayed as we listened to the witch doctor's chant as he performed a ceremony. The ceremony always included blood and usually ended with the patient drinking warm blood of the sacrificed animal—whether chicken, pig, or rat.

Juan and Eulalia had been close neighbors during those years. They differed from most families in that they had only one child. Eight-year-old Beto, an especially bright boy, was his parents' pride and joy. Beto had been among the first students to attend the new school.

One noon Beto ran home for lunch, but Eulalia had gone to the fleld and not yet returned. Beto had been warned never to play with fire, but he was hungry. He bent down, pushed

85

the ends of the glowing sticks together and slowly blew until they flamed up. Pleased with his accomplishment, he found the bean pot and put it on to heat. Then he ran out to play and forgot the fire.

Suddenly we had heard a shout and looked out to see Juan's hut engulfed in flames. The thatch roof and pole walls burned in minutes—taking with them Juan's entire coffee and bean crop which was stored in the house.

At sundown Juan and Eulalia had returned from the field and stared in disbelief at the pile of ashes that had been their home. Eulalia turned her back to the smoldering mound and cried. Juan picked up a stick and poked through the rubble. Neither scolded Beto, who stood alone and bewildered.

We invited Juan and Eulalia to live with us while they built another house. They were reluctant—but what could they do? Their relatives had large families cramped into small homes. They accepted our invitation.

Juan had been stoic in the loss of their home even though it was planting season and would be weeks before he could build another. Eulalia cried and wrung her hands. She refused to eat and became despondent. Most nights we heard her crying softly as Juan comforted her.

During one of those long sleepless nights, I got up to offer them a hot drink. Eulalia was crying and seemed even sadder than usual. As she sipped hot *ul,* she confided that she was pregnant and scared.

"I've been pregnant eight times, but only Beto was born alive," she said through her tears. "It's not Juan's fault that we don't have children. Each time, he paid Lencho to perform a 'live baby' ceremony. Lencho chanted, sprinkled blood in the corners of our house, and smeared my abdomen with blood. But nothing helped. All my babies died two weeks before time for them to see the world." Eulalia paused and wiped her eyes on her sleeve. Juan moved closer and patted her hand.

"And now I'm pregnant again," she said as tears rolled down her checks. "I want my baby to live. I don't want to bury another baby."

No one spoke. I heard Vi swallow and knew she was struggling with her emotions. I wiped my eyes, glad that the room was in semidarkness and that Beto was asleep.

My mind roved over medical conditions that could be responsible for so many stillborn infants.

After a few minutes Eulalia regained her composure and, in a barely audible voice, asked if I knew how to "see a baby into the world."

My first impulse had been to say no. But the tiny flicker of hope that led her to confide such deep hurts kept me from saying it.

As carefully as I could, I had explained that although her problem sounded serious, I knew a living God who loved us and listened to us when we talked with him. I couldn't promise her anything except that I would talk with him and ask him to help me know what to do.

During the next five months, day after day I went to Eulalia's new little hut. I listened to the baby's fetal heartbeat, prayed with Eulalia, and told her about the Lord. Since she assured me that each of her babies had died just before birth, I decided that if the fetal heart rate changed or the baby's movements became sluggish I would induce labor in an effort to deliver a live baby.

God had a better plan. He had kept the baby alive and well and gave Eulalia a safe delivery. The night little Marta was born, many close neighbors were awakened by her loud, shrill cry. No doubt they lay awake for a while wondering about the white woman who knew how to "see babies into the world." Perhaps they wondered, too, about their witch doctors, who had failed so many times.

Juan, Eulalia, and baby Marta often visited us. On one such visit when Marta was six months old, Juan sat cuddling her and stroking her tiny arm as Beto regaled us with his baby sister's accomplishments. Eulalia stared out the door, lost in thought. Then, with a faraway look in her eyes she said, "Just think, if years ago someone had told us about an Almighty God to whom we can talk, all my babies could have been born alive."

My heart skipped a beat. At that point we had lived in Chivalito for two years, and although we spoke Tila and had shared the gospel with many, no one had expressed any interest in it. But Marta's birth suddenly changed all that. At last—at long, long last—someone had acknowledged God!

If Marta's birth had a dramatic effect on Juan and Eulalia, it had an electrifying influence on the rest of the village. After two years of no medical work, I was suddenly flooded with it.

A week after Marta's birth, my afternoon translation session had been interrupted by excited yells and commotion. I looked out to see two men struggling under the weight of a body swinging in a hammock supported by poles resting on their shoulders. Several others hurried along beside the hammock calling instructions or giving encouragement.

I dropped my pen and hurried to the clinic just as Aureliano and Luis lowered the hammock to the floor. As the men gave a jumbled account of the accident, I slit the seam on Jeronimo's pant leg and exposed a deep, gaping six-inch machete wound. All talking stopped. Men craned forward to see the wound. The "oh's" and "ah's" told Jeronimo that the cut was bad. He tried to lift his head to see but changed his mind and lay still.

"Do you know how to fix it?" Santiago asked.

The men had heard about Marta. They wondered if I also knew how to treat other medical problems.

"The doctor in Salto sews skin with thread, just like a woman sews," Luis said.

They stood in awed silence as I injected local anesthesia and cleaned the wound.

"See, I told you she had a needle," Aureliano said with a satisfied smile as I opened a sterile package and took out a needle and suture material.

No one spoke. All attention was on the needle as I carefully sutured the wound.

Tenderhearted Felix closed his eyes and shuddered. He didn't want to watch. He moved up beside his friend's head. "Ah, Jero, doesn't that hurt?" he asked.

"No. I don't even feel it," Jeronimo assured him.

Old Nicholas's eyes widened. "It must be magic," he said in a low admiring voice. "Magic! That's what it is."

In spite of my explanation, the men assured each other that my fingers knew magic. A needle certainly hurt if it pricked the skin. Why, then, didn't this one hurt?

A few weeks after Jeronimo's accident, Felix had stood at our door holding out his hand with the severed tendons. The Lord used that tendon repair to not only change Felix's life but, in the course of the next eight years, also to change the lives of hundreds of Tilas. Within two months of Felix's conversion, Rosendo accepted the Lord. Soon after that Juan and Eulalia decided to turn their backs on the "old way" and follow the Lord. Santiago, who had watched from the sidelines, also stepped out and made the same bold decision. And on and on it had gone. Now, eight years after Marta's dramatic birth, there were hundreds of Tila believers.

89

On and on the merry-go-round spun. There was no end to important projects and programs affecting the lives and well-being of the Tilas. But always in the center of the wheel and uppermost on our minds, was the primary reason for our living in this isolated village. We were there to translate God's Word for these people. This was the *one* project that would have a profound and everlasting effect on their lives. Slowly and painstakingly, we continued the project.

"How did the translation of 2 Corinthians go this afternoon?" I asked as Vi and I sat down to a bowl of soup.

"Real good. I'm to verse seven of chapter three. How'd you do? Did you ever get out of the clinic?"

"Nope," I answered. "There was a steady stream of people—all emergencies that really needed help." I sighed and shook my head. "I'll never finish Hebrews at this rate."

"But the clinic is important, too," Vi consoled. "Both Felix and Juan were attracted to the Lord because of medical help. There wouldn't be much point in a translation if there were no Christians to read it," she added.

"I guess you're right," I said. "You know, when I was in high school there were two things I always dreamed about—living in a jungle and doing medical work."

"But now there's too much of it," Vi said understandingly. "Perhaps we need to ask the Lord to keep back the medicals so you can have time to translate."

"Yeah," I agreed with a sigh. "I know it's helpful and I enjoy it, but it's not my primary reason for being here."

The Lord understood my sigh. The translation program stayed on schedule in spite of ever-increasing medical responsibilities as I treated patients from seven surrounding villages. The three witch doctors in Chivalito not only became regular patients but occasionally brought their patients to me.

Injections became very popular, although often misunderstood.

"Do you have an injection for a toothache?" a young man from Pueblo Nuevo asked.

"How long has it hurt?"

"Oh, about a month. And it's all swollen like this," he said, moving his outstretched fingers to indicate a swollen cheek.

I looked again—his face wasn't swollen. "Let me see," I said as I moved closer and motioned for him to open his mouth.

"Oh it's not *my* tooth," he exclaimed. "It's my grandmother's. We live far away, so if you'll put the injection here," he said, pointing to his arm, "Grandma won't have to come."

Old Pedro, waiting to have his foot bandaged, looked up and snickered. "Shots don't work that way," he said. He paused, scratched his head, then tipping his chin in my direction, added, "She'll explain it."

Ten minutes later I convinced the young man that what Pedro said was true. With a shy grin, he bought the prescribed medicine and hurried out the door.

My microscope, which unfortunately added to the mystique of the clinic, helped in the diagnosis of a host of parasites. After isolating a parasite, I often let the patient look through the lens to see what was causing his problem.

"Hey, look!" he would exclaim. "This is what my stomachache looks like!"

I smiled—and stifled my impatience—as his friends, one after another, wanted to look at the offending "bug."

91

I discovered that when they saw the "wigglies" that made them sick, I could count on their cooperation to take the treatment.

Although medical work was time consuming, it paid rich dividends as I shared the gospel with patients. I also discovered how conscientious the believers were in sharing their faith. Patients who came from outlying villages were witnessed to several times before they reached the clinic.

Late one evening Vi and I were thinking ahead to the completion of the Tila New Testament. We had had a very good day—the final draft was almost finished.

"Wouldn't it be great to go to another language and start all over again?" I asked, with a stretch of the arms that included the whole world.

"Yes, it sounds great when we're this far along," Vi laughed, "but the first couple of years don't seem so great."

"It must be a little like having a baby," I chuckled, "painful when you're doing it, but wonderful when it's over."

We both knew that before leaving the Tilas, every aspect of the work must be in their hands. We had already made the transition in several phases of the program: the pastors and evangelists did a great job in nine surrounding areas; Chivalito deacons trained fellow deacons in new areas; Juan, the church treasurer, kept accurate records; Celia taught women's Bible classes; Adela and Basilia helped in the children's Bible clubs and would soon take over the leadership.

Many people in Chivalito now spoke Spanish. We arranged for a friend, a Mexican schoolteacher, to teach in the fall.

I trained five Tila women in midwifery. They did a fine job and won the respect and esteem of the village. I assured them that if they had a problem, I'd be glad to help.

92

Two years passed with no complications. Then late one Saturday afternoon, Carmen went into labor.

Maria, the midwife, had visited Carmen on a regular basis and arrived quickly when Jose called. Carmen's labor went smoothly, and she gave birth to a baby boy. But then the problem struck. The baby quit breathing!

In spite of all the well-practiced procedures, Maria could not revive him. In utter dismay, she laid the tiny body aside.

Jose sent for me, but before I arrived they faced another problem, Carmen hemorrhaged and slipped into unconsciousness. I administered two flasks of glucose and other emergency measures. Nothing helped. There was little hope that she would live until morning. Through the long night, Jose paced the floor and muttered to himself.

"Can't you make her live?" he pleaded. "Can't you make her wake up and talk to us?"

"No, Jose," I answered. "Her problem is different. Her only hope is if we can get her to the hospital—but she might not live, even then."

He glanced at the moon. "It will soon be daylight," he said. "We have to take her out. We have to try."

"No! You can't do that," Carmen's mother protested. "You should let her die at home. Why would you take her to a foreign place where her spirit will never find its way back?"

Then turning to me, she yelled, "You just want to take her out and sell her soul."

I sighed. I had arrived at Carmen's house before dark— now it was almost morning. I was physically and emotionally drained. But worst of all, I was trapped between a dying friend and a divided family. I knew the taboos and potential problems we would face if Carmen died while out of the village. Should I listen to a very distressed Jose? Did we dare defy Chula, Carmen's mother?

Neither Carmen nor Jose was a believer. Carmen was a good friend but always turned away at any mention of the Lord. Her brother, Carlos, was one of the village witch doctors. Chula was openly antagonistic to us and to the gospel.

At daylight Jose and I went out into the yard where we could talk alone. He wanted to take Carmen to the hospital.

"Jose," I said, "you must understand that Carmen is very sick. She might die before we can even put her in the plane or she might die in the plane, up in the air. Only God decides when a person lives and dies. I don't know which he has chosen for Carmen."

"Yes, I understand," Jose answered. "Rosendo told me about God. If God has chosen life for Carmen, we need to take her to the hospital so the doctor can help her."

We made the decision. At 7:30 A.M., exhausted and bedraggled, I hurried home, contacted the MAF pilot, and arranged the forty-five minute flight to San Cristobal de Las Casas.

The next days were dramatic and traumatic. As Carmen recovered, Jose accepted the Lord. His conversion was deep and genuine. Carmen accepted Jose's decision without comment but wanted no part of it for herself.

Three days later we returned to Chivalito. During my absence, Vi had prepared for our trip to Mexico City. From there she would go to Kansas to help her parents celebrate their golden wedding anniversary. We expected to return to Chivalito in one month.

Although I looked forward to a break in Mexico City, I hated to leave Carmen. She had gained strength but still rejected the Lord.

"I think I'll go see Carmen this afternoon," I said as we finished lunch. "She may not listen, but I'd like to talk with her about the Lord one more time before we leave."

"This may be a good time to do it," Vi said. "Chula went to Salto this morning."

When I arrived, Carmen was on a grass mat beyond a temporary partition in their hut. Carmen's married sister, Anita, who also staunchly opposed the gospel, was grinding corn. I spoke to her, then went behind the partition and sat down beside Carmen. "I want in tell you about the Lord again," I said. To my surprise, she nodded and told me to go ahead. As I talked, her nods became more enthusiastic. I soon realized that Anita had quit grinding, slipped out of the house, and was standing with her ear pressed to the pole wall, listening.

Carmen, engrossed in all I said, repeated each Bible verse after me. When I finished, I asked if she understood God's plan of salvation. Her answer was immediate. "Yes, I understood it all, and it felt good to my heart."

I prayed, then asked if she wanted to pray. Without hesitation she invited Christ into her heart. After praying, she looked up and smiled. "Talking to the Lord is wonderful," she said. "We should do that every day."

As I told Carmen good-bye and prepared to leave, Anita stepped back inside the house. "Let me walk you home," she said.

Walk me home? Our house was a short distance away, and I had walked that trail hundreds of times. As I opened my mouth to assure her there was no problem in my going alone, a little light flickered in my brain. I accepted her offer.

A few minutes down the trail, we stopped in the shade of a huge tree. "You were listening when I told Carmen about the Lord, weren't you?" I asked. "Yes," she said. "Jose talks about it a lot. I wanted to hear more."

"Did you understand what I told Carmen?"

"Yes. You said it just like Rosendo did last night. He and Jose came to tell Roberto, but I listened. I want Jesus to clean my heart and help me walk the straight path, just like Jose is doing," she continued.

She bowed her head and accepted the Lord. With a quick smile, she turned and hurried to tell Carmen the news. She forgot she was going to walk me home.

Upon our return a month later we found that Roberto, impressed by the change in Anita's life, had accepted the Lord. Carmen was well and she and Jose, accompanied by Anita and Roberto, attended church together.

All phases of the work had gone well: The new schoolteacher was doing a great job; the preaching, evangelization, and Bible classes also continued on track. Even the midwifery had proceeded smoothly. All had gone well except the medical work. As far as it was concerned, we were still at square one. That, too, must be put securely into Tila hands. We needed someone who was not only sharp, but also free to be trained over a long period of time. Surely the Lord had someone in mind. But who?

As we prayed about it, Vi and I noticed that Santiago's son, Margarito, spent a lot of time in the clinic. He attended two medical workshops I had given to train men from other villages. He had been among the first to give an injection as the men practiced in class.

One afternoon a few days later, I glanced out the window as Santiago and Margarito returned from the field. Astonished, I looked again. "Have you noticed how tall Margarito is?" I commented.

"Yes," Vi said without looking up, "he's not a little boy anymore. He's as tall as his dad."

I stared after them. It was true. Margarito, at sixteen, was a young man.

The next afternoon Margarito stood at my elbow as I prepared a slide for the microscope.

"Do you want to look at this one?" I asked, stepping aside. He bent down, looked through the eyepiece, and carefully examined the slide. Minutes later he isolated the hookworm.

He was right!

Suddenly I saw Margarito in a new light. Could he be the one the Lord had chosen to meet the medical needs of these people? Was he really interested in medicine, or did he just have time on his hands? Was he mature enough to handle it, or would he panic in the face of an emergency?

I decided to talk with Santiago. After all, eleven years ago Santiago invited us to Chivalito so five-year-old Margarito could learn marks on paper. Always at the head of his class, Margarito had fulfilled his father's dream.

The next day I talked with Santiago. He was awed and thrilled. "I think he would like to study medicine," he said. "He enjoys the microscope and talks about the way you sew cuts and set bones."

"Good! He might not learn to set bones," I said with a laugh, "but if he's interested in medicine, he could learn to do lots of things."

Santiago was strictly a "bottom line" man. "OK," he said, "I'll talk with him tonight. If he likes the idea, what do we do to get started?"

"Let's start by freeing him from the cornfield for a couple of months, so he can work with me during clinic hours," I

97

suggested. "In that length of time, he'll know if he really likes it, and we'll see how he does."

The next day Margarito arrived at the clinic with his hair slicked back and an I'm-here-to-tackle-the-world smile.

And he did!

Before two months passed, it was obvious that Margarito had an unusual talent for the work. He was fluent in Spanish and enjoyed medical textbooks. I prepared exams to cover each chapter. He studied hard and did well.

Two months stretched into nine. By then, he sutured wounds, prescribed medicine accurately, took charge of the microscope and lab work, and gave all types of injections.

The village was proud of its new "doctor." I was proud of him too. But most of all, I was grateful to the Lord for his faithfulness and perfect timing in preparing someone to assist in the medical work.

After years on the medical merry-go-round, the Lord let me off just as the final proofreading of the entire New Testament fell into our hands.

11
"I Feel Like a King On a Throne"

Being ahead of schedule was a unique experience for me. It was July 1974, and we had translated the entire New Testament and turned it in to the computer department in Mexico City. Month after month the final printouts piled up on our desks demanding attention. We proofread, corrected, and proofread them again.

Everyone knew that Fridays were reserved for translation. They all cooperated. Luis even kept his radio turned low on that day. To our amazement, non-Christians joined the others in keeping our Fridays free. They were not interested in the Scriptures but were intrigued by our ability to "stare at paper" all day.

Chivalito Christians kept a close tab on the progress of THE BOOK. We were surprised, however, when people from other villages took up the "how-much-longer-before-we-have-the-book?" theme. The almost unbearable heat and the drippy jungle humidity, coupled with the incessant question helped us make up our minds to take a translation helper to Mexico City, where we could work without interruption as we gave the New Testament its final polish.

The congregation chose Aureliano to make the trip with us. At a special prayer meeting, the church committed the three of us to the Lord and asked him to give us divine wisdom to make their book "perfect."

A week later, wearing the first pair of shoes he had ever owned and carrying a small shoulder bag that contained all he expected to need for a month, Aureliano, along with Vi and me boarded the MAF plane, and we were off on a great adventure. Although we knew his stomach must be swatting at swarms of butterflies, Aureliano showed no emotion as the plane rumbled down the short, grassy strip, lifted, and circled above the village. A crowd gathered to see us off and waved as the plane climbed higher. Aureliano smiled and waved back, unaware that they couldn't see him.

"Look how tiny the school is!" he shouted above the plane's roar. "And there's Rosendo's horse. It's only this big," he laughed as he held his hands a foot apart.

Our pilot Gene smiled and glanced at me. His passengers seldom enjoyed their first flight. We marveled but felt the worst was yet to come.

Others who stoically endured a flight came close to panic on their first car ride. They paled and covered their eyes as other cars hurtled down the street toward them!

But not Aureliano. He enjoyed his first ride and was full of questions about cars and what made them run. He grinned and commented on the variety of shapes and colors.

"Why did all the cars stop?" he asked suddenly as our taxi pulled up at San Cristobal's only traffic light.

As I finished my explanation, the light changed and traffic surged forward. "That's neat," he said, shaking his head in wonder. "Everybody knows how to do it. They all stop and go at the right time."

Aureliano took everything in stride: electric lights, telephones, television, running water, ice cream. Everything. Wide-eyed, he enjoyed it all.

On the jet flight to Mexico City, he was delighted with breakfast served on "baby tables" as we looked down on banks of fluffy white clouds. "So this is the way clouds look from the top side," he chortled.

He loved the Wycliffe headquarters with its electric gate, wide grassy lawns, and friendly people. We showed him the dining room, publications department, laundry, office buildings, and apartments. Since his room was in a different building from ours, we taught him to use the phone. Vi went to our apartment while I stayed in Aureliano's to dial her number. After a few brief words on the phone, he put it down, stepped to the door, and looked around. "So that's where Vi is, way up there?" he asked, pointing to an upstairs room across the campus.

"Uh-huh," I agreed.

He stood, craning his neck, his eyes scanning the distance. For the first time since we left the village, he seemed unnerved. "What does it?" he asked. "What grabs my words and throws them up there?"

Although my explanation was limited, he decided that phones must be all right if we used them.

"Do it again," I urged, "so you'll remember the numbers." Without hesitation, he dialed Vi's number and talked with her. A moment later, when she rang his number, he picked up the phone and continued the conversation.

His broad smile indicated that phones were now "old hat" to him!

A half hour later he knocked on our door. "Are you ready to work?" he asked. And work we did—hour after hour, day after day, for the next three weeks.

The computer printout of the entire New Testament was a foot-high stack of 8½ by11-inch spiral-bound notebooks. Our job was to check every word, every verse, and every comma and period from Matthew through Revelation. We felt a great weight of responsibility as we picked up Matthew and started that journey.

We decided that Aureliano, who was an excellent reader, would read aloud as Vi and I, red pens in hand, noted corrections.

Mark was the only Gospel we had printed as a separate portion. Aureliano enjoyed Matthew, Luke, and John. Occasionally he paused, reread a sentence, and changed a word from one position to another. He was quick to catch typographical errors that slipped past our eyes. Immersed in the account, he read chapter after chapter without tiring.

The book of Acts, first printed eight years before, was a favorite of the church. He read the revised pages with enthusiasm. "Hey, listen to that?" he beamed. "Peter was not afraid to preach, even after the rulers put him in jail."

Aureliano had an insatiable desire to read God's Word. He arrived early each morning and read until we were too exhausted to stay alert. It reminded me of the way I had felt years before when I slipped away from friends, went to the library, and secretly read the Bible.

On a couple of occasions, we suggested taking a few hours to visit a zoo or department store. "OK," he agreed, "but let's finish the next chapter first." When we finished that chapter, he quickly turned to the next, hoping we wouldn't put down our pens.

We had not printed Romans as a separate portion, and Aureliano had been out of the village the year we translated it. He had never heard the message of the book.

Late one afternoon we neared the end of the eighth chapter with its long list of concepts difficult to express in Tila.

Who shall separate us from the love of Christ? Shall tribulation, or distress, or persecution, or famine, or nakedness, or peril, or sword? As it is written, For thy sake we are killed all the day long; we are accounted as sheep for the slaughter. Nay, in all these things we are more than conquerors through him that loved us. For I am persuaded, that neither death, nor life, nor angels, nor principalities, nor powers, nor things present, nor things to come, nor height nor depth, nor any other creature, shall be able to separate us from the love of God, which is in Christ Jesus our Lord. (Romans 8:35-39)

At the end of verse 39, Aureliano paused and started over with verse 35. He read slowly as if pondering the meaning.

I glanced at the verses. Felix and I had worked hard to make the Apostle Paul's long, flowing narrative fit the Tila pattern of short, meaningful sentences. We had been pleased with the result. As Aureliano reread the passage, my mind raced ahead, searching for his problem.

He finished reading but didn't take his eyes from the page. I waited another minute but he didn't look up or speak.

Quietly I asked, "What's the problem, little brother? Do these verses not speak clearly?"

He lifted his eyes and nodded. "Oh yes," he said in a hushed voice, "they are beautiful. Just think, through Christ we are more than conquerors. Nothing—absolutely nothing that happens to us—can push His love away from us."

He reached out and tenderly touched the foot-high pile of printouts on the corner of the desk. With reverence in his voice, he said, "Ruby, I'm the first Tila man to have *all* of this book in my hand. I feel like a king on the throne as I sit here day after day and read God's Word."

That night I lay awake remembering the soft look in Aureliano's eyes and the awe and reverence in his voice as he read God's Word—God's Holy Word. What had happened to my heart? Had I become so used to reading that beautiful message that I no longer felt the wonder of it? Had I allowed some of the awe and marvel of the Book to slip away? How long had it been since I felt like royalty because I could read the most important Book in the world? Tears filled my eyes. "Oh God," I prayed, "make my heart tender toward you—tender toward your Word, the Living, Everlasting Word."

Ten days later, with Aureliano as vivacious as ever, we returned the polished New Testament to the publications department and headed south to our steamy jungle home.

A few people, who had become lax in their desire to read, now gave it their wholehearted attention. Everyone, it seemed, wanted to learn. Vi, excellent teacher that she is, was hard pressed to keep up with them. Could this possibly be the same village where eleven years before they stoned our house and scorned the very idea of "marks on paper"?

A few months later a letter from Mexico City informed us that the Tila New Testament was nearing the final stages of printing and would be shipped in June.

The jungle buzzed with the news. Christians met to plan the biggest Tila celebration ever held.

One day, amid such a backdrop of joy and anticipation, the MAF plane rolled to a stop on the airstrip. "Hello, ladies," Gene greeted. "I hear the great day is coming." He unloaded our regular monthly supplies and then reached for the mailbag. His hand came up empty. He scowled, stuck his head in the baggage compartment, and looked around. It was no use. The mailbag was not there. Our whole month's collection of mail had been left in the MAF hanger.

Gene apologized. I tried to smile—without much success. My face must have registered the disappointment I felt, for a dear little, illiterate Indian woman stepped closer, slipped her arm around my waist and tenderly patted me. 'That's all right," she whispered. "Does it really matter very much if you didn't get that big old bag of papers? You have the whole Bible. And you know how to read. And you can read it just any time you want to."

Somehow I got through the rest of the day, but that night I sobbed into my pillow. I sobbed for millions of people all over the world who didn't even have a written language, people who would never hold a Bible in their hands and read it. I sobbed too, because this was the second time in the last six months that my heart needed to be reminded of the riches I had at my fingertips—concordances, Bible handbooks, an atlas of the Bible, Bible dictionaries, and several volumes of Bible commentaries. But most important of all, sitting in a neat row on my desk was version upon version of the Bible. My cheeks damp with tears, I asked the Lord to make me as eager to read his love letters as I was the letters from friends at home.

The Lord is faithful and did a refreshing work in my heart that night. MAF, a tremendous organization that never before had forgotten our mail, flew over the village the next day and parachuted it to us. The school kids squealed with delight as the parachute filled and gracefully floated toward us.

So did I!

12
D-Day

D-Day (Dedication Day) was one week away, and Chivalito buzzed with activity. The large Christian community considered the arrival of God's Word the most important event ever to take place in the village. After years of waiting, *Jini Wen bu T'an* would be in their hands. They planned a huge celebration to welcome it.

The church rented a twelve-foot saw, carried it three hours over a mountain trail, and spent weeks cutting mahogany boards to serve as benches and tables. Two large, temporary shelters were constructed to provide shade for the special services and the feast to follow. For weeks, women and girls sewed new shirts and dresses. Many of them had raised a pig or turkey to provide meat for the occasion. Now they were busy shelling corn for tortillas as the aroma of toasting coffee filled the air. The children joined in the excitement and carried loads of firewood, which they carefully stacked under the shelter.

As if to add to the joy of the day, the MAF plane suddenly roared into view, made a low pass over the airstrip, and rolled to a stop in front of our house. "Hey, our New Testaments have arrived," the Tilas excitedly called to each other as they dropped their work and, coming from every direction, converged on the airstrip.

Their laughter and camaraderie suddenly subsided as Gene, looking concerned, climbed out of the plane. He solemnly greeted us and shook hands with those who crowded around, hoping for a glimpse of the long-awaited book. He waved to the others and walked toward our house.

"It seems there is a problem with your New Testaments," he began. "They were shipped on schedule twelve days ago but haven't arrived. For the last two days Linder and I and the Mexico City office have tried to trace them. So far, we don't have a clue where they are."

"How long does it usually take for a shipment to arrive?" Vi asked.

"Two days. But sometimes they're slow, so we gave them four before we inquired." He took a deep breath and continued. "It seems there may be more to it than just a misplaced shipment. Even the truck has disappeared without a trace."

"What about the driver?" Vi asked with sudden inspiration. "Hasn't he reported an accident or anything?"

"Nope. Nothing. He not only hasn't reported, but the shipping company can't even locate him."

"What does Linder think?" I asked, referring to Linder Tanksley, a veteran Wycliffe missionary who, in my opinion, had a knack for making big problems seem small.

Gene looked away. I knew he wished I hadn't asked that question. "Well," he stalled, "he did mention something that happened a few years ago. He said that a driver had an accident and was afraid the company would blame him. He left the truck on a side road and took off."

Gene paused and shook hands with a group of new arrivals. We sat still and waited for him to finish the story.

"A week later the company found the truck," Gene continued. "It had been looted. The shipment was never recovered."

"Looted? Looted—like everything stolen?" I said in a tiny, disbelieving voice.

Gene nodded.

A large crowd of Tilas pressed into the room. From Gene's demeanor and our anxious questions, they realized something was wrong. I glanced at Vi. Could this really be happening? Instead of happily unpacking the first copies of the published New Testament, we were being told that the entire shipment was lost.

Gene ran his hands through his hair and looked away as we explained to the Tilas. They were momentarily dismayed. All of their books lost? No, that couldn't be true. "The God-of-immeasurable-wisdom knows everything," they assured each other. "The books can't be lost. God can see where they are."

They felt there was no need to worry. They would talk with God. He would take care of the problem.

That evening, even as the congregation met to pray about the lost books, a tiny maggot of doubt wiggled in my brain. I put it down with a quick slap. It would be quite impossible to have a New Testament dedication without New Testaments!

Each morning several Tilas crowded around waiting for the 7:30 radio contact. Each morning Gene's message was the same: No books. Day by day, an increasingly large number of people reminded the Lord that the New Testaments had not been found. No one doubted that they would arrive on time.

The Christians continued preparations at full speed, including a morning and evening prayer meeting to thank the Lord that His Word would soon be in their hands. The celebration was two days away. The New Testaments were still missing.

In spite of the problem, Vi and I looked forward to seeing friends from the States. The Jake Friesens from Meade, Kansas, would represent Vi's home church. Rev. Kenneth Gage and Mr. Hershel Taber would come from Yuma, Arizona to represent mine. William and Margaret Van Wienen from Rockford, Michigan, who, along with children Marcia and Mark, had paid for the printing of the New Testament, would be on hand.

Al and Eunice Williams, Wycliffe friends, offered to meet the visitors in Mexico City and shepherd them to the village. Alice Beebe, who personally steered the New Testament through the publications department as it made its way from a rough manuscript to a beautiful hardback book, would accompany them.

Hank and Char Stegenga cut their furlough a week short to join us. The president of the World Home Bible League, the bishop of the State of Chiapas, and the president of Salto also planned to attend.

Late that night I lay awake staring into the dark. I heard Vi's bed squeak as she tossed and turned.

"What will we do if the New Testaments don't get here?" she asked.

"I don't know. There are still two days. People are praying, and everybody's working on it. They'll probably get here."

I heard her sit up in bed. "Do you suppose there has ever been a dedication service with no books to dedicate?"

"I doubt it," I said with a chuckle. "I don't think that will happen."

Several minutes passed. In spite of a very long day, neither of us was sleepy.

"Do you remember months ago when we first talked about the dedication?" Vi asked. "We said that we wanted a *unique* service."

"Yeah," I answered. "Unique because we didn't want to follow the custom of receiving a special leather-bound copy with our name on it."

"Well, we said *unique*. And it will certainly be unique if the books don't get here," Vi quipped.

"Well, in that case, I change my mind," I said, enjoying the banter.

Vi was quiet for a long time. I thought that perhaps she was asleep.

"Are you awake?" she asked softly.

"Uh-huh."

"I remember someone saying that Corrie ten Boom says 'God has no problems, only plans.'"

"Hey, I like that!" I answered with enthusiasm. "And I'm sure God has big plans for the Tila New Testament."

"I hope those plans include getting it here on time," she sighed.

The next day Felix, Rosendo, Arturo, and Marcial met with us to put the final touches on the program. Aureliano would be master of ceremonies; Felix would read a portion from the new Book; witch doctor Lencho's three grown sons, all vivacious Christians, would sing a special number; Ildefonso Pulido, the Mexican pastor who had aired our radio programs for six years, would attend and bring his church band.

We also decided that Felix, the Catholic bishop, and the president of Salto, representing Christians, Catholics and all others, would receive the only three New Testaments officially presented.

"I think we should give one of our books to Ruby's church and one to Vi's," Felix said with a broad smile. "They sent Ruby and Vi to write God's Word for us."

"And one to the Van Wienens," Marcial added. "They helped us, too, and they'll want to see it."

"And we'll all write our names in each book," Rosendo suggested as he held up a finger and wrote his name in the air.

All was in readiness—with one major exception. The New Testaments were still lost. And only one more day until D-Day.

The next day Gene's message was the same. No books.

The Tila New Testament dedication was indeed unique. It was done with ONE New Testament—a copy that Eunice Williams shoved into her handbag to show our visitors on the flight to Chiapas. She and Al knew the books had been lost but mistakenly heard that they were found.

During the dedication, that one copy was passed from person to person. Each lovingly fingered its pages and admired it. All who had saved twenty pesos to buy one went home that evening with the crumpled bill shoved deep in their pockets.

We watched our Tila friends, concerned for the many new Christians who had prayed that the books would be found in time. What would this do to their tender faith?

I had an answer sooner than I expected.

That evening, Felix, Juan, and Aureliano came to visit. They seemed happy and vivacious. A few minutes later I heard them talking with Lencho's sons and a group of new believers from Lumija. "The New Testaments aren't really lost from God's sight," Juan said. "God sees every hidden

111

comer. It's only that *we* don't know where they are. But we'll find them. Then we'll always have them to read and enjoy."

"It's sort of like eating wild pig," Aureliano explained thoughtfully. "When you haven't had meat for a long time, you get hungry for it. You start watching for tracks and hope you can find a pig. Then one day you capture one, and it tastes better than ever because you had to wait so long." He licked his lips at the thought.

"Yeah," Felix added with a laugh. "We've waited all our lives for the New Testament. We just didn't know we were waiting. Now we've tasted it and are hungry for more. We will feast on it when it comes."

Santiago joined the group. "It's God's Word," he observed in his no-nonsense way. "It's everlasting. It won't change just because we wait a little longer."

I stood for a minute, thinking about what I'd overheard. "Thank you, Lord, for letting me hear that," I prayed, pleased that disappointment had not shaken the Tilas' faith in God's love and care.

Although I didn't know it at the time, we later discovered that while we were concerned for the Tilas, they were concerned for us. Concerned that we would be sad or disappointed.

Aureliano, who had accompanied us to Mexico City, told them how differently we lived in the "big world." "In Mexico City they wear pretty dresses and shiny shoes that make them walk around on their toes. There's no mud out there; they walk on long cement paths.

"And they never carry water; it just comes out of long pipes. They turn a silver-colored handle and choose if they want it to come out hot or cold."

"Who heats the water in the pipes?" Margarito asked.

"I don't know," Aureliano answered, "but somebody keeps it hot, and there's always lots of it.

"And when they want to talk with a friend," he continued, "they don't walk to the friend's house. They feed numbers into a funny-looking machine, then sit in a big soft chair, and talk to someone who lives far away."

Santiago looked up with a puzzled frown. "What kind of machine is that? What makes it talk?" he asked.

"I don't know," Aureliano admitted. "Ruby couldn't exactly tell me. But somehow it grabs the voice and throws it to the other house." He shrugged. "Life is different out there," he concluded.

"But they like it in Chivalito," Margarito said.

"Yeah, they like it," Aureliano agreed, "but today their hearts must be sad. Their friends came from the big world to see their work, and there are no books to show them."

"You may be right," Santiago said thoughtfully. "But they don't look sad."

"No, they don't." Felix agreed. "But I think Aureliano is right. A corner of their heart must be disappointed, just like ours. Disappointed that we can't hold the book in our hands today."

Early the next morning Bill Van Wienen, Pastor Gage, and Al Williams stood watching a group of Tilas who had gathered around Ildefonso Pulido and his band. The band played hymns as the men laughed and sang together.

"It's hard to know who's having more fun, the Spanish speakers trying to sing Tila or the Tilas singing in Spanish," Bill commented with a smile.

"That's a special sight," Al said wistfully. "Those men from two very different languages and cultures met for the first time yesterday, and today they're like old friends."

Pastor Gage nodded. "We often say that the ground at the foot of the cross is level," he said. "Seeing three cultures merged together in a little Indian village proves it."

"Well, the New Testament didn't get into their hands yesterday," Bill observed, "but there is certainly evidence that its message is in their hearts."

After breakfast we said good-bye to Ildefonso and his wife, as well as several Tumbala Indian friends who came three days over the trail to be with us.

After they left, MAF pilot Ross Drown helped Gene airlift us and the visitors twenty minutes over the jungle to the village of Limar for a second day of celebration.

Limar, a day away by trail, had been evangelized by Felix and Aureliano. As people turned to the Lord, they discipled them, taught them to read Tila, and helped them establish a church. We had often prayed for the Limar people by name but had never met them. They knew us as "Ruby and Vi, the bringers of the Word." We looked forward to our first visit to the Limar church.

As Ross taxied to a stop in Limar, his radio suddenly crackled with a wonderful message. "The New Testaments have been located!"

The Limar service was performed with the same copy of the New Testament we had used the day before. But there was a great difference. During the service, Ross flew to San Cristobal de Las Casas and brought back a load of books.

Two hours later, Limar Christians thronged the airstrip as Ross rumbled to a stop and unloaded several boxes of the precious cargo. They lined up with their twenty peso bills and became the first to own a copy of the Tila New Testament—the book that could make them feel like a king on a throne.

That afternoon, back in Chivalito, we discovered that a very strange thing had happened. The New Testaments that Ross delivered to Limar were the *only ones* that had been found!

Linder Tanksley was not home when the books were delivered to his house. His daughter Susi could only say that a taxi brought them. She didn't know who or from where.

Our joy was short-lived; we were back to square one. The Limar Christians had bought all the available books; there were no more New Testaments—and no clues where to look!

Possibly Felix had the only acceptable answer to the day's puzzle. "The believers in Limar are very young in the Lord," he said. "They probably would not have understood if they had prepared a celebration to welcome the books and the books had not come. It's good that the New Testaments went to them." Marcial and Rosendo, standing nearby, nodded approval.

I glanced at Vi. We had known these three men before they became Christians. I marveled at the grace of God that softens and changes a human heart.

The next morning Ross and Gene arrived to fly the visitors out. Vi hugged Margaret Friesen and said, "I'm glad you came but sorry you didn't get to see Chivalito receive the New Testament."

'That's all right," Margaret said with a soft look in her pretty brown eyes, "It's better to see it in their hearts than in their hands. We're proud of you girls and the way the Lord has used you."

Margaret Van Wienen, standing beside me, turned and gave me a warm hug. "Bill and I want to second that!" she said.

Minutes later, the plane roared down the muddy airstrip and lifted into a bright blue sky. As we watched, it circled and tipped its wings in a good-bye wave.

The visitors were gone. The celebration was over. The New Testaments were still lost.

A week after the visitors left, the shipping company found the missing cargo. The truck had turned over about half way to its destination. Its contents were retrieved and stored in various warehouses of a large Mexican food chain in the state of Oaxaca. The books indeed had been well hidden.

That Sunday Felix led the church in a service of thanksgiving. Many people became the proud owners of a bright new book with shiny gold letters on the outside and a life-changing message on the inside.

Several people, however, had to wait much longer for their New Testaments, for they arrived simultaneously with a measles epidemic.

Measles is a "foreign disease" and often takes a dreadful toll in an Indian village. Over the next few days, more than a hundred people contracted measles, and many of our close friends hovered between life and death. Before it subsided, the epidemic claimed the lives of several children and two outstanding young men, both active in the Lord's work.

Domingo, cousin to one of the men who died, did not contract measles but suffered in a different way. Days passed as his wife, Basilia, and their two small children remained in a critical condition.

As one agonizing day slipped into another, Domingo killed a chicken and forced broth down feverish throats. He bought medicine with the twenty pesos he had saved for a New Testament.

Each time Domingo came to the clinic, he sat for an hour and quietly read my copy of the Tila New Testament. Then with a sigh, he solemnly closed it and placed it on the shelf. There was no money to buy one, and he didn't want to be in debt.

One morning three weeks later, Domingo bounded into the clinic with a wide smile. He pulled two twenty peso bills from his pocket, laid them down, and picked up two New Testaments as gently as if they were fragile. Standing there, lost in thought, he idly ran his finger over the gold letters on the black cover. At last! At long last, he owned that wonderful book.

As he wrapped his prized possessions in a clean cloth, I quietly said, "Little brother Domingo, I'm happy that you have your book. Where did you get the money to buy two?"

He smiled and said, "Basilia is much better. Last night she was able to talk. 'You know,' she said, 'we have eaten lots of chicken these last weeks. It tasted good with *swelux* (wild onions) and *juc* (a root vegetable). But even as good as it tasted, a week later our stomachs forgot that we ate it. It made us strong, but now we have only two chickens left. If we were to sell a chicken and buy God's Word, reading and believing it would make our children strong for all of their lives,' she said.

"We talked for a while and decided to sell both chickens and buy two New Testaments," Domingo continued. "Basilia needs one at home. Mine will be walking the trail as I go to other villages with Felix and Rosendo."

He gave the books a final caress and slipped them into his bag. With a spring in his step, he hurried home.

Almost daily, Tilas came from far and near to buy a New Testament. Within weeks half of the once-lost shipment had found its way into Tila homes. Each became a treasured possession, as the family gathered around a flickering open fire in the center of their dirt-floor home and listened to the ever-new message of the Savior.

The measles epidemic was past.

D-Day, with its joys and disappointments, was past.

The Word of God in the Tila New Testament was there to stay.

13
On a Hilltop Looking Back...

Chivalito Christians had trudged endless miles of jungle trails to share the joy of their new faith. The Lord blessed those efforts. Over the past five years, eight Tila churches were established as hundreds of men and women trusted the Lord to "turn their hearts around and help them walk the straight trail."

But this new little church, high on a hilltop in Francisco Leon, had a special place in my heart—this church had been built by witch doctor Lencho's family and friends.

Vi and I arrived early that morning. From our vantage point beside the new church, we watched as group after group of happy, chattering Tilas stopped at the rushing stream far below and splashed water over their muddy feet before making their way up the steep hillside. They were too far away for us to understand words, but their festive mood was obvious as they laughed and teased.

I watched and wondered if anyone else was remembering that dreadful day four years ago when Lencho had been murdered six feet from our door.

"Does it seem possible that it was four years ago that Lencho was murdered?" Vi asked, as if reading my thoughts.

"Yes, I guess so if you stop to remember that Abram was a new believer at that time and is now a preacher," I answered thoughtfully.

We stood, idly watching three teenaged boys scramble up the hill. Neither of us spoke. The morning was cool, and the sun felt good on my back. I took a deep breath, enjoying the smell of meat roasting on an open fire.

Although Vi seemed absorbed in watching the boys, she suddenly grimaced and looked away. I knew she was reliving the grisly murder.

"You know, sometimes I still see and hear that whole experience as if it were yesterday," she said, shuddering.

"I know. I do, too," I responded, thinking back to that frightful afternoon when Vi and I had been jarred from our translation desks by an angry shout outside our door. I had dropped my pen and stepped to the window just in time to see the flash of Pedro's razor-sharp machete slash through Lencho's head. The sight and dull crunch were locked in my brain forever.

I had been too stunned to turn my head or even close my eyes as the second and third angry swish of the nineteen-inch blade severed one of Lencho's arms at the shoulder and split the other hand into two wildly flinging halves.

Pedro quickly sheathed his bloody machete and hurried down the overgrown trail. At last he had settled a long-standing dispute.

Lencho lay bleeding to death at our doorstep.

But today, in spite of the reminders all around us, I pushed the memories away. This was a special day, a long-awaited day. Today two hundred Tilas from five surrounding villages were joining Lencho's sons to dedicate to the Lord a beautiful balsa-pole church that stood less than thirty feet from Lencho's old house.

Lencho's three grown sons, Abram, Gomercindo, and Marcelino had lived in a cluster of homes around their father. A year before their father's murder, one after another, the three young men turned to the Lord. Lencho listened as his sons shared the exciting truths they learned from the Word.

But mostly he just watched. Abram, about twenty-five and the oldest, looked, talked, and acted like his father. He, like his father, had spent much of his time drunk. Would belonging to the Christ they talked about change that? Lencho would wait and see.

Gomercindo borrowed a Gospel Recordings phonograph, and family members took turns cranking the handle. The records, referred to as 'black tortillas that talk," clearly presented the gospel message. Lencho often joined the family group as they gathered to listen.

The village of Francisco Leon was a two-hour walk from Chivalito. Each week Arturo and a group of men conducted a church service in Abram's home. Neighbors, attracted by the singing, often sat around on rocks and stumps in the yard. As months passed, several accepted the Lord. Their lives changed as they listened to God's Word and followed its teaching. Abram and his brothers were sure that their father and his two wives would also believe.

As more people in Francisco Leon expressed interest in the gospel, the three brothers realized they needed a building large enough to accommodate the growing crowd.

Then came the awful day of the brutal murder.

According to Tila tradition, Abram, as the oldest son, was responsible for finding his father's murderer and avenging the death. But Abram was a new creature in Christ—a tiny baby still on a milk diet. His heart barely fathomed the things of the "straight trail." Suddenly, in one dreadful moment, he was expected to take a sharp detour from that trail.

He stood irresolute, wavering between his duty as a son and his conviction as a Christian.

"Don't give us any of your 'straight trail' talk," a neighbor screamed in derision. "Your father was a powerful witch doctor, and it is your duty to find Pedro and kill him—cut him in pieces like a butchered pig."

"Do it today," another shouted. "Are you going to cower behind a book, or are you going to be a man?"

Abram's eyes flashed with anger—anger at Pedro for killing his father—anger at his father's friends for taunting him. They were right. It *was* his duty. He would kill Pedro.

Several Christians spent that first awful night with Abram and his brothers. They prayed and read Scripture with them. They encouraged them to trust the Lord and walk with him.

By morning the first hot flashes of anger and dismay had passed. The brothers agreed to abandon Tila tradition and follow the Lord. They would ask the authorities to find Pedro and punish him.

Lencho's friends were bitter; they felt Abram had betrayed his father. Gomercindo tried to reason with them. "God's Word teaches that murder is wrong," he said. "It is as wrong for Abram to kill Pedro as it was for Pedro to kill our father."

"Women!" the friends shouted, shaking their fists. "All three of you are useless women who don't know how to use a machete."

Salto authorities knew Lencho. They made one feeble effort to find Pedro and then ignored the murder. "He was just another witch doctor; probably deserved what he got," they reasoned.

Time helped erase the brothers' pain and disillusionment. It also erased the anger and frustration of Lencho's friends.

Today, four years later, as I stood on the hilltop and looked at the remains of Lencho's home and all the things that had made up his little world, I marveled at the changes the gospel had made in the lives of his family and friends.

After the murder, the three brothers had continued to grow in their understanding of the Word as Felix and others made weekly trips to Francisco Leon. After a few months, Abram and Gomercindo began taking turns reading aloud as the family group gathered each night. Gomercindo had a special gift for understanding and sharing God's Word. Felix was pleased. "Someday Gomercindo will be an outstanding preacher," he said with a satisfied smile.

Gomercindo's wife was the first of the women to ask the Lord to turn her heart around. Within weeks, Abram's wife and Lencho's two widows made the same decision.

The group of believers grew to seventeen as several men joined the three brothers in their walk down the "straight trail."

Each night still others gathered in the wide empty yard to enjoy the singing. Abram and Gomercindo were excited. "We should think about a church again," Abram said one evening after the group left.

"Yes, we should," Gornercindo quickly agreed, remembering the effort that had been interrupted by their father's death. "It's hard to listen while sitting on a stump out in the yard," he added.

"A bat swooped over our heads all evening," teenaged Alejandro piped up. "The men laughed and swatted at it, but no one could hit it."

"Our houses are very small. It would be nice to have a church,' Lencho's widow said with a melancholy nod. "I think everyone would help build it."

Almost two months later, with the building begun, the measles epidemic that had passed through Chivalito spread to Abram's hilltop. Before it passed, Gomercindo, the promising young preacher, was dead.

The village of Francisco Leon was grief-stricken and bewildered. "Who is this God they continually talk about?" one of the old men asked. "Why isn't the family angry at him?"

"How can Gomercindo's mother continue to smile when her son is dead?" the women wondered.

Abram sat and read the Tila New Testament. He seldom spoke. He and Gomercindo had always been very close. They had accepted the Lord at the same time and together had shared the gospel with their neighbors.

With Gomercindo gone, would Abram give up? Would the building project that they had so happily begun, continue? We prayed for Abram and the gospel testimony in Francisco Leon.

Each evening for the next two weeks, Chivalito Christians made the two-hour trek to Abram's home to pray with the family and encourage them in the Lord. A group of about twenty neighbors often gathered in the yard as Abram and the Chivalito men talked about the Lord and Gomercindo's new home in heaven.

One evening two months later, when Arturo and the Chivalito group arrived to conduct a service, Abram and . about twelve men were working on the half-completed church building. With a somber smile, Abram said, "Rainy season is coming and people won't be able to sit under the stars and listen as we preach God's Word. Many want to hear about heaven. We decided to complete the building."

And today—the building completed—we stood on that hilltop with two hundred Tilas to dedicate it to the Lord.

The day sped past. The messages were good and the singing exceptional. There were frequent references to heaven and Gomercindo.

In the late afternoon a rustle of movement from across the aisle caught my attention. A group of people from another village nudged each other and prepared to leave. I glanced at my watch. It was 4:30.

"Did you bring a flashlight?" I whispered.

"No, did you?" Vi asked. I shook my head.

Darkness comes early in the dense jungle, making travel difficult over narrow trails crisscrossed with roots and hanging vines.

"Maybe we should go," I whispered, thinking of the two rivers we had to cross, and the muddy conditions we had battled that morning.

"OK," she responded, "but let's wait a few minutes. With that group leaving, Abram may realize that it's getting late."

We settled back and waited. Within minutes, the visiting pastor concluded the message, and Abram called Felix forward to offer the dedicatory prayer. The congregation stood and sang "Trust and Obey." By the time we finished the last verse, the people who had prepared and served food, tended fires, carried water, and did a multitude of other jobs that made the day a success, pushed their way into the already crowded building. The song leader swung his arms as a signal, and the congregation sang the hymn a second time. The volume increased, and the two hundred voices sounded like four hundred. I'm sure the Lord enjoyed the adoration that spiraled heavenward.

Walking stick in hand, Vi and I joined the Chivalito group and started down an almost dark trail. Two hours later, wet, muddy, and in the pitch dark, we straggled up to our door. Inside, with the lamp lit, we looked at each other and burst out laughing. "Hey, it looks like you're starting a new style," Vi teased, touching my dress, which was muddy to the waist.

"Yep. Straight from Paris. It's called 'moonlight mud splash,'" I laughed.

125

We sat down, pulled off our muddy shoes and gratefully soaked our feet in a basin of water.

"What do you think Pastor Gage would say if he could see you right now?" Vi smiled.

"Probably check my sanity," I quipped. "But this was a wonderful day, wasn't it?"

"Yes, it was," Vi agreed. "That's a very pretty little church. And just think it's on the *very property* of the man who once boasted that be could completely destroy the Christian testimony among the Tilas!"

14
Amen

The night had been a short one. When I awoke, I lay still and let my mind replay the happy scenes of yesterday's church dedication.

I heard a giggle outside our door and realized that Marta and Pedro were patiently waiting for us to get up so they could wash our muddy shoes in a nearby stream. A piece of bubble gum was the reward for clean shoes, and Marta and Pedro were keen competitors to see who could blow the biggest bubbles.

I pushed the mosquito net aside and rolled out of bed. Little did I realize as I opened the wooden shutters and looked out on the lush green hillside, that that would be the last Sunday Vi and I would spend in Chivalito for almost two years. Before another Sunday rolled around, an urgent message would call Vi home to help care for her mother through a long, debilitating illness. I'm glad that the Lord in his omniscience kept it from us that morning as I handed Marta and Pedro our shoes and watched them scamper down the jungle trail.

By eight o'clock our front room, which people referred to as their "house," filled with men who arrived early for a village business meeting. The village of Santa Lucia, although forty-five minutes away by trail, was considered part of the "Chivalito *ejido*," and the men from there were expected to attend the Chivalito meetings.

Margarito, who had assumed much of the growing medical work, arrived to dispense medicine to the Santa Lucia men while they waited for the meeting to start. Others crowded into the house. A large group shared our three view masters and chatted about the colorful slides of Mexico City. Several converged at the bookshelves that occupied a prominent place on one wall. Someone put a Tila record on a Gospel Recordings phonograph and cranked out the message. A few listened, but others laughed and talked loudly as if to drown it out. It reminded us of the services during our early years in Chivalito. In those days, Felix was often one of the loud ones. He later explained that one got laughed at or ridiculed for openly listening to the gospel. The way to avoid ridicule was to talk loudly and pretend to pay no attention. We wondered how many of the Santa Lucia men being loud today really had hungry hearts.

As the morning progressed a number of men arrived on horseback, and our backyard became their "parking lot." It was hard to realize that less than five years ago Rosendo had owned the first horse in the village. After Rosendo finally got his horse back, it became a trendsetter. Lencho, who had stolen the horse as part of his grand scheme to wipe out the Christian testimony, was dead. Yesterday we attended the dedication of a beautiful church that stood a few feet from his old house. Lencho's widow was among a group of recently baptized Christians who would take communion for the first time in today's church service.

The village business meeting finished by noon. After a quick lunch, we picked our way to church over the muddy trail. The building quickly filled, and people sat around in the large, grassy yard. For several months the church had used a battery-operated amplifier to join the outside congregation with the inside one.

There had been much discussion about how to enlarge the building. In the end, however, it was decided to build a new church and to leave the old building for Sunday school rooms, women's meetings, and children's Bible clubs. The women were thrilled. Many of them had found the Lord during the women's Bible studies and had an emotional attachment to the church.

Basilia and Adela were the new leaders of the women's Bible study and were doing a good job. The Lord had given Arturo and Adela a baby girl following their infant son's death when the owl flew into their house. Arturo, who had been the shyest one in the first preacher-training class, was now the pastor of the Chivalito congregation. He was not only an excellent preacher but also played the guitar well.

Arturo had always enjoyed the guitar music on Pastor Pulido's radio program, which preceded our Tila program. One day he saw a guitar in Salto and bought it. Although he had never seen one before, he asked the Lord to help him learn to play. Evening after evening he picked at the strings until notes began to fit melodies. Soon he was playing hymns. A short time later Alejandro and Domingo also bought guitars and the church rang with music. Arturo taught Adela, and music became a great attraction at the women's weekday Bible study.

Basilia, who helped Adela with the study, owned a New Testament of her own—the one bought with their last chicken when she and the children were recuperating from measles. That New Testament was a wonderful investment. Basilia not only loved to study but also was a good teacher. Could it really have been such a few short years ago that the entire village considered it a waste of time for girls to "know paper?"

Vi and I were also glad that the church was left intact. Often during a service I enjoyed looking up at the galvanized metal roof and worshiping the Almighty God, who hears our prayers and keeps his promises. I believe he enjoyed adding a special, personal touch to this little church when he gave new Christians wisdom to put up that roof without a single nail hole. I enjoyed every service as I quietly praised the Lord for the church and the humble Tila Indians who had become my brothers and sisters in Christ.

But the church was now definitely too small. By two o'clock the congregation had assembled, and we were wedged into place on the backless slab benches. I was glad the Tilas are clean people. Most smelled of smoke from their open fires, but many smelled of bath soap bought in Salto with money that formerly would have been spent for liquor.

Some people, who insisted on being inside, were standing. Custom dictated that men sit on one side and women on the other. There were always more men than women, so several extra benches were squeezed in on the men's side, and their seating arrangement was even tighter than ours. To further complicate things, small children often crowded in with their fathers while their mothers held a new baby.

I looked around. No one seemed to mind the crowding. All were anticipating the service.

The guitars were finally tuned. Arturo stood and announced the first hymn. Marcial, the song leader, flipped through his hymnal and found the page. All was quiet for a long moment; then, in a beautiful, loud voice on perfect pitch, he started the hymn. The guitars, one after another, joined in, and by the time we reached the end of the first verse, the entire congregation was singing. The building rang with the sound of joyful hearts worshiping God. I glanced across the aisle at Marcial, a handsome young man with a very special talent.

As we sang, I remembered how Marcial had first been attracted to the gospel through hymns. His brother-in-law, Felix, had often witnessed to him, but Marcial either went out of his way to ignore Felix or to otherwise make it clear that he had no interest. Then one day when Marcial went to Felix's house to visit Petrona, he came upon their little five-year-old Timoteo "conducting a service" in their yard. Marcial quickly stepped back among the trees and listened. Timo, unaware that anyone was listening, continued the "service." He owned a well-worn copy of an old *Reader's Digest,* which served as both his hymnal and his New Testament during family devotions. He propped his book on a burned-out tree trunk and turned the pages from time to time as he sang scattered bits of one hymn after another to a very puzzled flock of chickens. Then Timo closed his book, bowed his head, and prayed. The service over, he grabbed the *Digest* and scampered off to other things.

Marcial, deeply touched by Timo's prayer, decided he wanted to hear more about God. He started going to church but, to keep his interest a secret, crouched well back in the dense jungle growth where he could hear without being seen. After weeks of secretively listening to the Word preached, Marcial made a bold, life-changing decision and became a "new creature in Christ."

My mind wandered from the congregational hymn as I thought about the many ways the Lord had worked in hearts to draw these people to himself.

Marcial's father, Pascual—a known murderer—had never shown any interest in the gospel. Although it had taken him several months to get over the embarrassment of having to trade another daughter to old Moises in place of Petrona, he had finally accepted Felix as a good son-in-law. Almost a year later when Felix accepted the Lord and became the first Tila believer, Pascual wasted no time in letting the village know how he felt about that! Within a few years, however, he realized that Felix and Petrona were more content and happy than he had ever been. When little Timo talked with his grandfather about the Lord, Pascual's heart became tender toward God.

Pascual's early disdain for God had been shared by Carmelino, Felix's father. Carmelino's god-shelf was the biggest and most ornate in the village. He expected Felix, as his oldest son, to assume the responsibility of keeping the shelf decorated with flowers. Felix's conversion to the Lord had left Carmelino bewildered and embarrassed.

"Son, the way of our ancestors is the only true way," Carmelino had gently counseled. "You should forget all this foolishness about a living God. It can't be true. It's just a strange idea the foreign women have brought to Chivalito. You'll see."

Carmelino, however, was the one who had changed his mind.

Felix's deep love for the Lord and his quiet, consistent testimony won Carmelino's interest—and eventually his heart. Almost eight years after Felix turned to the Lord, Carmelino asked the church leaders to join him as he removed the family god-shelf from his home.

As I relived the happy memories of that day, I glanced across the aisle at Carmelino. Today he had on a new plaid shirt, and in spite of the heat, the long sleeves were neatly buttoned at the wrists. He smiled and held out his hand. His grandson Timo squirmed his way among the men to find a place beside him.

The hymn was over, and I automatically sat down, still thinking about Carmelino. My reminiscing heart had started on a trip, and I was having trouble concentrating on the service.

Arturo's voice, resounding on the amplifier at the back of the church, brought me back to reality.

"Aureliano is back from a weeklong evangelistic trip to Chupija," he said, speaking into the microphone. "We'll ask him to come forward and bring us up to date on what's happening over there."

I looked up as Aureliano pushed past the men on his bench and made his way to the front of the congregation. The New Testament in his hand seemed a part of him as he opened it and read several verses. As I listened, I remembered the weeks we had spent in Mexico City, where, hour after hour, we proofread the Book. Aureliano obviously still felt like a "king on a throne" to have the New Testament in his hands.

After his report, several prayed for the new Christians in Chupija, who were undergoing persecution because of their faith in the Lord.

I fought back a surge of emotion as Santiago prayed. I remembered the evening several years before when he, as a new believer, pushed through a crowd of visitors in our living room and, without preamble, asked what God's Word said he should do to someone who had cut the ears off his biggest pig and threatened to do the same to him if he didn't quit following the "foreign women's way." That night the room had suddenly become hushed. Many of those present had faced a similar problem, but Santiago was the one to put it into words.

On that night, those six years ago, the Gospel of Matthew had not yet been translated into Tila. As I reached for my English Bible, I silently asked the Lord to help me share Christ's answer from Matthew 5:44: "But I say unto you, Love your enemies, bless them that curse you, do good to them that hate you, and pray for them which despitefully use you, and persecute you."

Everyone was quiet as I finished the spontaneous translation of the verse. After a minute or two, I began to wonder if they had understood. I looked at the verse again. Maybe I had not made it clear. Then Santiago, in his typical straightforward fashion said, "OK. That's what the Bible says. I'll do it. Let's pray right now. But you first. I'll pray for them because the Lord says to—but *you* ask God to help me love them."

And love them he did! And now, in response to Aureliano's report, he was praying for those he had never seen—those who lived in faraway Chupija and were taunting the new believers in that village just as he had been taunted.

As Santiago ended his prayer and the congregation sat down, I was again aware of the overcrowded church and the stifling heat. I glanced around. No one else seemed to notice. All were absorbed in the service. I silently thanked the Lord for the privilege of worshiping him with people who were so thrilled with his presence that neither jungle humidity nor severe overcrowding could rob them of their joy in him.

Suddenly Vi jerked and shifted her feet. Basilia, sitting beside us, reached down and grabbed up two-year-old Rosita who had been playing quietly at our feet. Rosita had just poured a big handful of sand into Vi's shoe. Now the bench was even more crowded as Basilia held her wiggling daughter on her lap. Vi reached over and gave her a little pat that said, "Don't worry. It's OK."

Since this was communion Sunday, several of the leaders who were often on evangelistic trips were home. Felix stood up to conduct the communion service. As he gestured the deacons forward, I caught a quick glimpse of the livid scar across his palm. I vividly remembered the day a broken liquor bottle had slashed the tendons of that hand. My reminiscing heart relived those long weeks of therapy that finally saw the hand useful again—and Felix's heart on the "straight trail." Felix had been the first to make that life-changing decision. But that had been twelve years ago. Since that time some 1,500 others had joined Felix and were following down the same trail.

There was some shuffling and changing of seats as the deacons moved forward to take their places behind the homemade communion table. My eyes roved over the group of humble, barefoot men standing before me. These were men who loved the Lord with all their hearts and had suffered much for the sake of the gospel, men who a few short years ago had been illiterate, machete-swinging drunks. I bowed my head and fought to control my emotions. How could one ever find adequate words to praise the God who makes such dramatic changes in hearts and lives? A favorite Tila expression came closer than English. They often referred to God as the "One-whose-greatness-cannot-be-measured."

The overcrowded church was hushed as the deacons began passing the communion bread. Then deacon Juan was beside me. As I reached for the bread, I glanced up and caught Juan's quiet smile. Miracle-baby Marta now had a three-year-old brother. Little Pablo had wiggled away from Eulalia's side and joined his father in the aisle as he passed the communion plate from row to row.

That minute, with no warning, my mind did the ultimate back flip of reminiscing as a startling thought hurled itself through my brain. How many of these quiet Christlike men had actually been part of the utter terror that had plagued our first weeks in Chivalito? My eyes again picked out Felix, Rosendo, Marcial, Arturo, Juan, Luis, Aureliano . . . Were these men, who today were serving us communion, among those who had pushed and shoved our doors and windows in a futile effort to break in? Were these men among those who had stoned our house and made such desperate efforts to force us from the village? Yes, surely they were!

My eyes filled with tears and the group blurred. God himself had performed this miracle—the miracle of new life in Christ.

The bread and grape juice was slowly distributed to all, including those seated on the grass in the yard. The deacons reassembled at the communion table, and Rosendo led in prayer. "Thank you, Lord," he prayed, "that we can talk with you, the one whose love is too great to be measured. Thank you that you love us and have made us yours. Lord, we love you with all our hearts. Amen."

As with one voice the entire congregation responded with a hearty "Amen."

Lost in thought, I looked around again at the evidence of that great love—at people whose lives had changed; people who loved the Lord and loved each other; people who, in spite of taunts and ridicule, walked endless miles over tangled, jungle trails to share that love with those who didn't even know they needed to hear it.

The congregation stood quietly as Marcial announced the final hymn. Without opening their hymnals, they joined him prayerfully as his deep, resonant voice rang out:

> My Jesus, I love thee, I know thou art mine,
> For thee all the follies of sin I resign;
> My gracious Redeemer, my Savior art thou
> If ever I loved thee, my Jesus, 'tis now.

As the sound of the last words faded, Felix raised his hand and pronounced a benediction. I'm sure heaven echoed my heartfelt AMEN.

*****

And Today...

The number of Tila believers has surpassed the four thousand mark and continues to increase.

Felix heads a committee of twenty active evangelists who, week after week, plod the jungle trails as they continue to sow the Seed.

There are a total of forty-eight Tila churches in widely scattered villages throughout the Tila area.

Tila radio programs continue unabated. Under the supervision of Arturo, several pastors and singing groups regularly make a trip to Macuspana, where they record that month's programs.

The first printing of the New Testament has sold out, requiring a second printing of two thousand books.

The Tila Old Testament Summary, a hardcover companion volume to the New Testament, has made the Tilas feel as "rich as kings" as they study God's Word.

The Tila concordance of the New Testament, published in 1981, is a valuable help to the believers as they share God's Word with others.

And Also

Vi, who returned to the States in 1977 to care for her parents until both passed away, has been serving Wycliffe in Dallas, Texas, as assistant editor of *Notes on Translation* in the Publications for Translators Department since 1983.

Ruby, who continued on in Mexico until 1980 in order to complete the Old Testament summary and to compile a Tila concordance, now serves as Director of the Conservative Baptist Released-time Programs among Navajos in Arizona.

Typical Tila home constructed of balsa poles that are tied in place with bark or vines.

Ruby contacting MAF base via battery-operated communications radio.

Felix, the first Tila believer, talking to Vi.

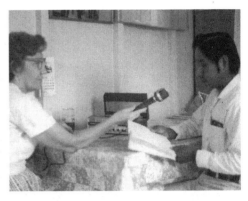

Aureliano, "a king on a throne," recording a Tila radio program.

Andres listening to the gospel via the "black tortilla that talks."

New Christians are proud of the first Tila church with its galvanized metal roof "winking in the sun."

Domingo, converted witch doctor, who said, "I'll go back and tell them again."

MAF plane on the airstrip in front of Ruby and Vi's home in Chivalito.

Tilas joyfully receive the New Testament.

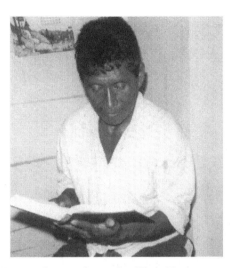

Rosendo reading the New Testament.

Visitors at the New Testament dedication (front row l. to r.):
Rev. Kenneth Gage, Eunice Williams, Margaret Friesen, Vi
Warkentin, Felix, Ruby Scott, (back row l. to r.) Hershel
Taber, Al Williams, Jake Friesen, Van Wienan family—
Margaret, Mark, Marcia, and Bill.

Made in the USA
Lexington, KY
02 December 2019